Grace Muigai

My Journey Through A Wilderness

By
Grace Muigai

PUBLISHED by PARABLES
Earthly Stories with a Heavenly Meaning

Grace Muigai

My Journey Through a Wilderness
Grace Muigai

Published By Parables
September, 2020

All Rights Reserved. No part of this book may be reproduced or utilized in any form or by any means, electronic or mechanical, including photocopying, recording, or by any information storage and retrieval system, without permission in writing from the author.

    ISBN 978-1-951497-91-0
    Printed in the United States of America

Readers should be aware that Internet Web sites offered as citations and/or sources for further information may have been changed or disappeared between the time this was written and the time it is read.

My Journey Through A Wilderness

By
Grace Muigai

Grace Muigai

MY JOURNEY THROUGH THE WILDERNESS.

Table of contents	1
Endorsements	3
Acknowledgements	4
Why I wrote this book	5
Wilderness	9
Types of spiritual wilderness	17
Is wilderness important?	29
Suffering that produces character	35
How to recognize your friends during the wilderness	48
What to pray for during wilderness	59
Performing other duties during wilderness	69
Choosing to overcome	75
Marching to victory	85
Receiving the glory	95
Remaining a winner	107
Maintaining the glory	117

Grace Muigai

ENDORSEMENT

In this book, *My Journey Through The Wilderness*, you will learn very many valuable lessons. I have walked the same journey with the author who also happens to be my spiritual daughter and a closest friend too. Many a times, she would call me or even pay me visits for just what I would call, 'shoulders to lean on'. She faithfully went through trials and if I may say here, I was challenged by her faith. She knew it would not last forever as if change was coming the following day. These are lessons that can be learnt by any other Christian out there.

Thank you, Grace, for keeping on even when times were particularly difficult for you. I call you a great soldier. God bless you.

                         Shelmith Wanjiku Nderitu.

ACKNOWLEDGEMENTS

I thank God for standing with me all through my life. He helped me manage though the difficult times. God will remain my strength, my joy, my Rock of salvation all the days of my life.

I thank my family too for being there for me. My husband Joseph, the love of my life and his constant encouragement. My wonderful children, Ann, Pendo and Juanita. I feel your support in every way.

My friends and spiritual supports like Shelmith Nderitu, Mrs.Elizabeth Maina and many others.

Finally, my father, in the faith, Prophet Shepherd Bushiri. So far yet so near. I love you in every way. How God sent you in my life at a time when I needed someone like you will forever remain a mystery. May God bless you Papa and Mama too Prophetess Mary Bushiri.

WHY I WROTE THIS BOOK

Many of us have in one time or another faced some crisis in life. It might have been an easier one that went for a day or a few days, then somehow were able to overcome. To others it might have been a very long period that was coupled with distress and frustrations. Whichever the case, none of us wants to lose; for loosing means that we are done. It also means that we have given in to the demands of the enemy hence loosing that precious testimony. We focus unto the calling of our God, which to us is so dear to lose. However, we might want to encourage those who have not yet made it.
The bible calls us 'more than conquerors'.

Romans 8:37-39
Yet in all these things, we are more than conquerors through Him who loved us.

38 for I am persuaded that neither death nor life, nor angels nor principalities nor powers, nor things present nor things to come,
39 nor height nor depth, nor any other created thing, shall be able to separate us from the love of God, which is in Christ Jesus our Lord.
NKJV

The reason for this is because it is Jesus who conquered for us and we enjoy the fruits of the pain of Jesus. When I was young, I used to watch the wrestling programs and one preacher would illustrate the scripture above and compare it with wrestlers. He would tell us that the man in the wrestling match fights hard against his opponents but when he wins the match, it is his wife and children who enjoys the big amount of money. Therefore, the wife in this case would proudly say that she was more than a conqueror, for she herself did not wrestle but she is enjoying the fruits of another man's pain.

When we are sons of God, we are bound to find many and tough obstacles in life. They are life hurdles that must be jumped high enough not to trip or fall back. The pain is felt in jumping but God assures us success. It is important to pay the price of righteousness for in due course, we are glorified.

Mostly, we suffer when we choose to resist the enemy. He afflicts us because he does not want to see us prosper. He sends us afflictions of every kind.

However, thanks to our GOD WHO IS MIGHTIER than him. HE wins over him and causes him to be downtrodden. That is why we must connect ourselves to God. Our God wins all battles. Do not doubt. He can win even in your case, which seems so mighty in your eyes. Do not give up. Pray until something happens. Seek wisdom from God alone. God may use His people to encourage and lift you up. You are important to Him and you matter. Do not worry over the many days, months and years the devil has ruined your peace, marriage, finances, and your relationship with your children and your parents.
Joel 2; 25-26 assures us of that.

25 So I will restore to you the years that the swarming locust has eaten, The crawling locust, The consuming locust, And the chewing locust, My great army which I sent among you.
26 You shall eat in plenty and be satisfied, and praise the name of the Lord your God, Who has dealt wondrously with you; and My people, shall never be put to shame.
27 Then you shall know that I am in the midst of Israel: I am the Lord your God and there is no other. My people shall never be put to shame.
NKJV

God is a restorer. He will restore to you the years that the enemy wasted in your life. Note He says He will restore the years that the canker worm has eaten. The enemy worked hard to destroy your years. He delayed you in accessing your blessings. He put blockages in your pipes that bring your benefits and ensured that you suffer so much. Praise be to God, He will restore all that.

He says that you shall eat in plenty, be satisfied and praise the Name of your God. You shall never be ashamed again.

Hallelujah! Desire to win. Desire to fight the good fight of faith.

1Timothy 6:12
Fight the good fight of faith, lay hold on eternal life, to which you were also called and have confessed the good confession in the presence of many witnesses.
NKJV

Lay hold on eternal life. Our God is true and does not change or even lie to us. His promises are ye and amen. I hope that as you read the following chapters, your strength is going to be renewed in the power of His might and that you are going to be an over comer. God bless you.

1.

1.
WILDERNESS

Before I got married, twenty years ago, I would never have imagined that I would experience some battles like the ones that came my way. They were all started by horrible dreams, which were very frightening. In one particular case, I dreamt with a gang running after me with machetes intending to kill me. I run and found a land protected with a barbed wire. I do not know

how I was able to gather my courage and strength and I jumped over the perimeter wire. The gangs still running and baying for my blood discovered I had jumped over but they themselves were not able to jump over. Most of these frightening dreams always ended with me in a very safe place and that gave me a lot of comfort. My marriage was in trouble and we frequently quarreled over anything. It would be over salting food, pair of socks thrown all over, finances, and children. Etc. However much we fought, we still held on to it. We had a way of showing people that we were okay yet deep inside ourselves, things were crumbling down. When I could not pretend anymore, I packed my belongings and moved out with our two young baby girls by then. My husband who could not bear to stay without his children would frequently come to visit us and that separation just proved to us how much we loved each other. It was a difficult period. We did not know how we would get out of this mess. We blamed each other. We did not know what enemy was fighting us. This was a very dry period for us. Luckily, by God's grace, we were able to get back together although it was not the end of our tribulations.
We were in our own wilderness.

A wilderness is an area of wild uncultivated land; an area where plants especially weeds grow in an uncontrolled way. Words that could be used in the place of wilderness are uninhabited region, inhospitable region, uncultivated region, jungle and desert. All those words try to explain to us that one cannot be comfortable in the wilderness. There is no joy and satisfaction in the wilderness. None of us would choose to stay in the wilderness. None of us would choose to stay in an inhospitable region. There is fear, trouble and frustrations of all kinds.

Acts 7:29-30
When Moses heard this, he fled to Midian, where he settled as a foreigner and had two sons. After forty years had passed, an angel appeared to Moses in the flames of a burning bush in the desert near Mount Sinai.

Moses had been raised in a royal palace. When it came time for him to identify with his Hebrew brothers, he acted impulsively. He needed to spend time in the wilderness to mature and to learn how to deal with people who were not raised in riches. During these forty years, Moses learned how to deal with shepherds. Since the nation of Israel was a nation of shepherds, this was extremely important. Sometimes, God lets us spend time in preparation. There may have been times when Moses felt he was wasting his life on the backside of the desert, but God had a plan for him. He needed to learn how to deal with the everyday occurrences of normal life.

Perhaps you feel like your life is being wasted. Remember, that even during those times in the wilderness God is teaching and preparing our hearts. There is an interesting Aesop's Fable called The

Traveler and the Plane-Tree, "Two Travelers, worn out by the heat of the summer's sun, laid themselves down at noon under the wide spreading branches of a Plane-Tree. As they rested under its shade, one of the Travelers said to the other, 'What a singularly useless tree is the Plane! It bears no fruit, and is not of the least service to man.' The Plane-Tree, interrupting him, said, 'You ungrateful fellows! Do you, while receiving benefits from me and resting under my shade, dare to describe me as useless and unprofitable'?"

You may feel that what God is taking you through is useless and unprofitable. However, there is benefit that you just cannot see or understand yet. If you are willing to place your full trust in God, you will discover that it is during those times that seemed the least important that God was preparing you for his best. When the children of Israel were in the wilderness, they complained and complained. Even when God told them not to complain, they continued, a thing, which displeased the Lord. They did not just complain but the reason was that life in the wilderness was very bitter. It was so uncomfortable that they actually forgot their reasons of leaving Egypt. Egypt was associated with hard labor and ruthless taskmasters. This people cried to God until He chose to deliver them. They were God's own people and that is why God had mercy upon them.

Exodus 3:7-9

7 And the Lord said: "I have surely seen the oppression of My people who are in Egypt, and have heard their cry because of their taskmasters, for I know their sorrows.
8 So I have come down to deliver them out of the hand of the Egyptians, and to bring them up from that land to a good and large land, to a land flowing with milk and honey, to the place of The Canaanites and the Hittites and the Amorites and the Perizzites and the Hivites and the Jebusites.
9 Now therefore, behold, the cry of the children of Israel has come to Me, and I have also seen the oppression with which the Egyptians oppress them.
NKJV

God promised to take them to the land of Canaan, a land flowing with milk and honey. *V.8* This people mattered to God. That is why He could not ignore their cries. He decided to deliver them from the hand of the Egyptian master. God picked out Moses and made him the leader and the deliverer. Why did God pick Moses? He was thoroughly trained in the wilderness to handle the job. Great assignments require great training sometimes in great wilderness. God's college is very peculiar. He clue it himself and does not promote you till He sees to it that you have gone through the wilderness to acquire the desired qualifications.
The day dawned and the Israelites walked out. God promised to be with them, to lead them during the day by a cloud and during the night by fire.

Deuteronomy 1:33

33 who went in the way before you to search out a place for you to pitch your tents, to show you the way you should go, in the fire by night and in the cloud by day.
NKJV

The Lord also provided bread, which rained from heaven as their food. They were not satisfied with these and therefore their complains again caused God to send manna to them. This manner was like coriander seeds (white) and the taste was as wafers made with honey. This is truly amazing. It says of the manna that 'it was white',

Exodus 16:31
And the house of Israel called its name Manna. And it was like white coriander seed, and the taste of it was like wafers made with honey.
NKJV

It also appeared as 'a layer of dew around the camp'. As it dried,' thin flakes like frost appeared on the desert floor.' Its initial appearance was as something 'white' and 'wet'. Only later did it dry and look like frost. As the dawn broke each new day and the Israelites scanned the ground to see if God had provided manna, they would be reminded of milk. Actually, manna looked like the real thing-milk and tasted like the real thing 'honey' but was not the real thing. It was just 'thin flakes' like wafers and so would not actually satisfy being in the real sense that it was not the normal ingredients of a good and satisfying meal.

The fresh provision of manna every morning, which in its appearance and taste of honey, reminded them of the real thing-the land flowing with milk and honey. God also gave them meat inform of quails when they complained of meat.

Nehemiah 9:20-21
You also gave your good Spirit to instruct them, and did not withhold your manna from their mouth, and gave them water for their thirst.
21 Forty years you sustained them in the wilderness; they lacked nothing; their clothes did wear out and their feet did not swell.
NKJV

They were sustained with that meal for forty years. However, to sustain is not to satisfy, and although the manna contained the whole balanced diet, it did not satisfy them and left them grumbling. They looked over their shoulders and wished for an opportunity to go back to Egypt. Even after God trying to create a picture in their minds concerning how Canaan was like, they still complained against God and wished to go back. Sometimes, we appear satisfied where we are until God shakes us from our comfort zones and takes us out of them. When He does that, we grumble because our human nature does not love pain or discomfort. Our God's plans are good. They make us grow and mature even spiritually.

Jeremiah 29:11-13
For I know the thoughts that I think toward you, says the Lord, thoughts of peace and not of evil, to give you a future and a hope.
12 Then you will call upon Me and go and pray to Me, and I will listen to you.
13 And you will seek me and find me, when you search for Me with all your heart.
NKJV

For the children of Israel to go to Canaan, a land flowing with milk and honey, they had to pass through the wilderness. Among the many places mentioned, includes the wilderness of Zin, Sinai, Eastern wilderness and others. Every time that we have to enjoy some prosperity, we have to be taken through some periods of hunger, desperation and other problems. It appears as if God just designed it that way. I understand that God is communicating to us a very powerful message during the wilderness. I am a teacher by profession. I studied English Literature and Music in college. That is what I teach today. I am a master at what I went to study in College. Spiritually, I am a master at what I have been tested through the wilderness. In the coming chapters, we shall explore briefly how some people like Joseph became a vice pharaoh in Egypt, Moses became a leader of the Israelites etc after going through a wilderness. If one is in a financial wilderness, God later puts them in charge of a financial entity. He teaches them to take care of His flock. If one is in a marital wilderness, God later helps them to assist those who are going through marital turbulences. Interestingly, some people are just afraid to go through a difficult period so they opt to stay where they are. Again, some blessings may not come to us, until God has pruned us enough to be able to handle them.

2.
TYPES OF SPIRITUAL WILDERNESS

Matthew 4:1-11

1. Then was Jesus led up of the Spirit into the wilderness to be tempted of the devil.

2. And when he had fasted forty days and forty nights, he was afterward an hungered.

3. And when the tempter came to him, he said, if thou be the Son of God, command that these stones be made bread.

4. But he answered and said, it is written, Man shall not live by bread alone, but by every word that proceedeth out of the mouth of God.

5. Then the devil taketh him up into the holy city, and setteth him on a pinnacle of the temple,

6. And saith unto him, If thou be the Son of God, cast thyself down: for it is written, He shall give his angels charge concerning thee: and in [their] hands they shall bear thee up, lest at any time thou dash thy foot against a stone.

7. *Jesus said unto him, it is written again, Thou shalt not tempt the Lord thy God.*
8. *Again, the devil taketh him up into an exceeding high mountain, and sheweth him all the kingdoms of the world, and the glory of them;*

9 And saith unto him, All these things will I give thee, if thou wilt fall down and worship me.
10 Then saith Jesus unto him, Get thee hence, Satan: for it is written, Thou shalt worship the Lord thy God, and him only shalt thou serve.
11 Then the devil leaveth him, and, behold, angels came and ministered unto him.

In this story, Jesus is driven into the wilderness at the start of his ministry. He is fasting and so he is very hungry. He encounters wild animals. After a 40 day ordeal, the angels come and wait on him, and filled with the Spirit, he continues into his ministry. This episode comes immediately after his baptism, where the voice from heavens has declared 'this is my beloved Son with whom I am well pleased'- an experience of blessing followed straight after by time in the desert. I take from this story that this experience is important to the journey of Christ and His followers- times of connection, empowerment, and recognition, as well as times of tiredness, temptation, and difficulty. Jesus re-enters the world having overcome his demons, his fears and temptations, having wrestled with uncertainty, pain and doubt. He is ready for his ministry. Readier now, than if he had gone straight from his baptism into his encounters with ordinary people while floating on a holy cloud.

Isaiah 45.3 says 'I will give you the treasures of darkness and riches hidden in secret places, so that you may know that it is I, the Lord, the God of Israel, who call you by your name.'

The desert is indeed a dark and lonely place. But if we can move through it, and stay with it, and eventually emerge from it, there is a hope that we will emerge with treasure, with jewels- of insight, of strength, of depth, of wisdom- hard won, and precious to us and to God.

Prophet Elijah has just engaged in some mighty acts of faith and firecrackers, which have put his life at risk, and he heads into the wilderness.

1 Kings 19
1. And Ahab told Jezebel all that Elijah had done, and withal how he had slain all the prophets with the sword.
2. Then Jezebel sent a messenger unto Elijah, saying, so let the gods do [to me], and more also, if I make not thy life as the life of one of them by tomorrow about this time.
3. And when he saw [that], he arose, and went for his life, and came to Beersheba, which [belongeth] to Judah, and left his servant there.
4. But he himself went a day's journey into the wilderness, and came and sat down under a juniper tree: and he requested for himself that he might die; and said, It is enough; now, O LORD, take away my life; for I [am] not better than my fathers.

5. *and as he lay and slept under a juniper tree, behold, then an angel touched him, and said unto him, Arise [and] eat.*
6. *and he looked, and, behold, [there was] a cake baked on the coals, and a cruse of water at his head. And he did eat and drink, and laid him down again.*
7. *and the angel of the LORD came again the second time, and touched him, and said, Arise [and] eat; because the journey [is] too great for thee.*
8. *and he arose, and did eat and drink, and went in the strength of that meat forty days and forty nights unto Horeb the mount of God.*
9. *And he came thither unto a cave, and lodged there; and, behold, the word of the LORD [came] to him, and he said unto him, what doest thou here, Elijah?*
10. *And he said, I have been very jealous for the LORD God of hosts: for the children of Israel have forsaken thy covenant, thrown down thine altars, and slain thy prophets with the sword; and I, [even] I only, am left; and they seek my life, to take it away.*
11. *and he said, Go forth, and stand upon the mount before the LORD. And, behold, the LORD passed by, and a great and strong wind rent the mountains, and brake in pieces the rocks before the LORD; [but] the LORD [was] not in the wind: and after the wind an earthquake; [but] the LORD [was] not in the earthquake:*
12. *And after the earthquake a fire; [but] the LORD [was] not in the fire: and after the fire a still small voice.*
13. *And it was [so], when Elijah heard [it], that he wrapped his face in his mantle, and went out, and stood in*

the entering in of the cave. And, behold, [there came] a voice unto him, and said, what does thou here, Elijah?
14. And he said, I have been very jealous for the LORD God of hosts: because the children of Israel have forsaken thy covenant, thrown down thine altars, and slain thy prophets with the sword; and I, [even] I only, am left; and they seek my life, to take it away.
15. and the LORD said unto him, Go, return on thy way to the wilderness of Damascus: and when thou comest, anoint Hazael [to be] king over Syria:
16. And Jehu the son of Nimshi shalt thou anoint [to be] king over Israel: and Elisha the son of Shaphat of Abelmeholah shalt thou anoint [to be] prophet in thy room.
17. and it shall come to pass, [that] him that escapeth the sword of Hazael shall Jehu slay: and him that escapeth from the sword of Jehu shall Elisha slay.
18. Yet I have left [me] seven thousand in Israel, all the knees which have not bowed unto Baal, and every mouth which hath not kissed him.
19. So he departed thence, and found Elisha the son of Shaphat, who [was] plowing [with] twelve yoke [of oxen] before him, and he with the twelfth: and Elijah passed by him, and cast his mantle upon him.
20. and he left the oxen, and ran after Elijah, and said, Let me, I pray thee, kiss my father and my mother, and [then] I will follow thee. And he said unto him, Go back again: for what have I done to thee?
21. and he returned back from him, and took a yoke of oxen, and slew them, and boiled their flesh with the instruments of the oxen, and gave unto the people, and

they did eat. Then he arose, and went after Elijah, and ministered unto him.

Straight after he makes his first complaint, Elijah goes straight to sleep. He is exhausted from his battle with the false prophets, and from the fear and disappointment that now plague him. Being in the wilderness, even if it is a primarily mental or emotional experience, can be physically tiring. Wielding emotional energy leaves us physically tired, as anyone who has been in counseling can attest. We need to be kind to ourselves, and allow for rest. Before any kind of conversation with Elijah, or spiritual renewal, God looks after Elijah's physical needs- for food, and drink, and yet more sleep. It is possible to over-spiritualize our needs and our experience, and sometimes, our first priority should be to take care of our physical wellbeing, to give us the strength and resilience to face the inner journey ahead. A little exercise, good sleep and good food can go a long way in the desert. If the desert is combined with depression, I strongly recommend a visit to the doctor for medication, and to a counselor to begin to work through the issues. These things won't necessarily resolve the sense of alienation from God, or the disconnection from faith…but they can create the conditions for more helpful engagement with the spiritual issues.

Elijah travels further into the wilderness, 40 days and nights, to speak with God. These 40 days are symbolic linked to the 40 year wandering of the Israelites in the desert (wilderness) before entering in the Promised Land, and implying a long, and spiritually purposeful time. There is a process of pilgrimage associated with the desert- there is a journey we have to travel, and sometimes it is only at the depths, and after much wandering, that the encounter or the shift occurs that moves us out of the desert. A really valuable part of that pilgrimage can be to get away from normal life for a bit, out of town, **Or to a retreat centre even if for one day..** Getting out of the normal rut of life can create a really helpful perspective… especially if the desert we are in is one caused by stress and busyness. Elijah tells his story- his hurt, angry, fearful and self-pitying story- to God, and he tells it twice. This suggests something important to me that sometimes we need to keep telling our story over and over, until a shift happens. God is robust enough to hear our anger and our disappointment as often and as forcefully as we need to say it. I think it is also a really good idea to find another person, or a small group, to tell about what is going on. Someone who can listen – not judgmentally, without trying to fix things, but who can pray and check from time to time, about how things are going.

Elijah also discovers that God is not in the fire or the earthquake or the rushing wind, but in the silence. God is not just in the major stuff or the events that are often considered significant but, also in the small moments the quiet moments, when grace comes to us. That means that in the desert, it is important to create this moment where we can be still, even if we have no expectation of God's presence, and can't or don't want to pray. The stillness can allow some things just to settle a bit, and enable us to pay attention to what is happening in our lives. These are the things I take from the biblical passage. Firstly, it can be really helpful to learn some strategies for praying without words, or in someone else's words. Often in the desert, words are problematic – we say something and then don't know if we really believe it, or our words seem thin and stupid compared to our experience. Or the very idea of prayer is impossible, because God has vanished. Prayer can include just sitting still, breathing ... maybe imagining, breathing in peace and breathing out the anxiety or hurt. Prayer can be sitting, listening to music. It can include reading prayers written by other people, rather than having to speak in your own words. Secondly, I think it can be important to take note of the oasis – when and where are the timing glimpses of God and grace and hope? Recording this to look over in the dark times can be helpful and thirdly, if church services are a difficult, painful, or just a plain boring place to be during wilderness, take a break and do not come for a while. However, maybe see if it is possible to replace the church service with some activity that does connect you to God... or what nourishes your spirit in some way....a walk in the bush, or meditation or some creative expression. A word of advice here, It is not a good idea to make too many significant life decisions while in the desert as it (desert) can distort your entire perception and can make other areas of life that are actually okay seem worse than they are.

The bible often depicts the experience of God's presence or blessing with the symbol of water-oasis etc. so it makes sense that times of distress, doubt and alienation from God are described with the symbol of desert or wilderness. The wilderness is where the wild animals live. Water is scarce. A traveler walks alone, in the heat and the cold, without shade or protection. It is a vulnerable place. In a spiritual wilderness, God feels far away. Faith feels doubtful or uncertain. The watery things that used to inspire and refresh us – worship, the bible, prayer etc become dry, meaningless, yielding nothing but dust to our weariness. We feel alone, vulnerable, lost and unprotected. There is fear too and one cannot help thinking such thoughts like Christianity is all bullshit, maybe I am unlovable, maybe God has forgotten or abandoned me, maybe I have wasted my life, maybe I am unspiritual, maybe God is a cruel and a misunderstanding monster. Like I said at the beginning of this book, some of us have been there in the past and came out of it, some of us are there now or maybe we will all go there again, or for the first time in the future.

The spiritual wilderness feels differently for different people – for some, the desert is a place of intense and devastating loss, for others, it is associated with a feeling of blah, humdrum, listlessness. It can last for a few days or for years. For some people, the experience of a spiritual desert leads to permanent loss of faith.

Christian faith and practice are put aside and never picked up again. For others, the wilderness forces a change of faith, re-framing and re-defining what Christianity means to them. Others emerge the other side of the wilderness with their faith intact pretty much as it was before, but with a renewed sense of refreshing and energy. Still others stay in the church because of various commitments, but remain in some low- grade wilderness for the rest of their lives. They come to believe that the possibility of a dynamic deep and nourishing faith is either a false expectation or is just not for them.

There are many kinds of wilderness and multiple reasons why we might end up in one. For many people, dismantling previous beliefs and assumptions about God and Christianity is a process that leads to turmoil and pain, and to a sense that there is nothing left, no thread of belief or hope. There is the wilderness of boredom, or the rut, when nothing inspiring or challenging has closed our paths for many years and our Christian vision has dimmed. There is the desert caused by fatigue, stress and overwork. Often what we experience as a spiritual wilderness has a mixture of physical, psychological and spiritual factors thrown in, and sorting out these threads is part of moving through this desert. Sometimes, the physical situation creates the spiritual one.

Illness and depression can lead to wilderness. When we are depressed or sick in some other way, our connection to God often disappears…and often the feeling of abandonment by God compounds the intensity of the depression. Shock and loss can plunge us into a desert – sometimes after a delay. Often, after a trauma or bereavement, others rally around, and a sense of God's comfort is very near and immediate. Our own defenses kick in to shield us from extent of the hurt we have sustained but as the time goes by, we find ourselves living in the desert of ongoing grief. This desert can be filled with anger at God, or an inability to see how any of the claims made by the Christian faith about God's love and care can be true.

Other reasons that may lead to wilderness include failing of exams, separation and divorce for married couples, a couple without a child due to barrenness, lack of finances to meet various needs, among many others. Our way in and our way out are unique to our specific circumstances and personality.

Is God with us in the desert too?
I cannot prescribe any quick solutions for escaping the desert but I may have some hard learned and wonderful insights about life in the desert to offer especially some that I gathered when I was in the wilderness too. One helpful thing to do is to name and accept of being in the desert. If I am in the desert, that is where I am. And just to acknowledge this can be a huge relieve, and can give a sense of peace in the midst of a situation other than fighting the waves that threaten to drown us or meekly sinking under them,

acceptance is a strong action that says 'I am in water that I did not want or chose but since I am here I will roll with the waves, keeping my head above water and maybe there will be a wave that I can surf all the way to shore.'

Accepting that I am in the desert also means accepting that this is where I might be for a fair amount of time – I don't need to scurry around for the fastest exit. While I do not think it is a good idea to rest permanently in the wilderness, it might be helpful if we resign to the fact that speedy exit out of it might not be in the offing. We need to move fully through our deserts, facing whatever we need to face. It can be helpful to try to identify what kind of a desert you are in…and if possible, why you are there. That might give some handless to the kind of process that is needed to move forward.

Another thing to know in the wilderness is that God is in the desert with us.

Psalms 23:4-5 records that for us.
4. Yea, though I walk through the valley of the shadow of death, I will fear no evil: for thou [art] with me; thy rod and thy staff they comfort me.
5. Thou preparest a table before me in the presence of mine enemies: thou anointest my head with oil; my cup runneth over.
God is not just on the other side of the desert waiting for us or back where we first entered it. God is right

there in the midst of it all. We may not be able to feel that, or to trust it. But we may at least be able to hold it as a possibility, as we journey. Also, we are not alone in terms of other people, either. While it is true that our experience is unique to us, there are others who have walked and are walking through a wilderness that is similar. We can develop an art of listening to others and what they are going through, and that should sustain us and give us hope to go on.

3.
IS WILDERNESS IMPORTANT

When I was in High School, I had a friend called Chichi. She was a very promiscuous girl and often was in trouble with the authorities for her lose morals. She would sneak out of school at night and go to discos in the nearby town. In a sad turn of events, Chichi contracted gonorrhea and really suffered for a long time before she was treated. When she finally got her healing from that disease, she learnt her manners and vowed never to misbehave again. She later accepted Jesus as her savior and she became very instrumental in the peers club. Some problems that happen to us do so to help us become careful with ourselves. Like what the psalmist says;

Psalms 119:71
It is good for me that I have been afflicted, that I may learn Your statutes.
NKJV

Psalms 119:75
I know, O Lord, that your judgments are right, And that in faithfulness you have afflicted me.
NKJV

Psalms 119:107

I am afflicted very much; revive me, O Lord, according to your word.
NKJV

It is not normal for one to confess like this unless one discovers the real reason and will of God; that one of changing him according to His purpose. God is a sovereign Lord. He wants us to learn His ways and to know Him in a very personal way. In most cases, He will allow us to go through a wilderness in order to correct our ways. He is also very jealous. He hates to see us being ignorant of His ways. Therefore, He will make us go through any kind of situation to correct us.

Jeremiah 18:1-6
The word which came to Jeremiah from the Lord, saying:
2 "Arise and go down to the potter's house, and there I will cause you to hear my words."
3 Then I went down to the potter's house, and there he was, making something at the wheel.
4 And the vessel that he made of clay was marred in the hand of the potter; so he made it .Again into another vessel, as it seemed good to the potter to make.
5 Then the word of the Lord came to me, saying:
6 "O house of Israel, can I not do with you as this potter?" says the Lord. "Look, as the clay is In the potter's hand, so are you in my hand, O house of Israel!
NKJV

God is in the business of remolding us all the time so that we can perfectly fit and meet the kingdom requirement. When the Israelites got into the wilderness, they realized that God did not want them to complain and grumble. Remember that grumbling had been their way of life in Egypt. It had been easy for them to be delivered from Egypt but practically hard for Egypt to be delivered from them. Hard work and mistreatment caused them to complain. That was normal to them. However, in the wilderness, God wanted them to trust Him. He wanted them to believe that a day would actually dawn when they would find themselves in Canaan. Their complains made God to delay their arrival to Canaan for a very long time in the wilderness. It was a journey they would have taken a period of eleven days but they ended up taking forty years.

It is all right when you tell God your troubles but He wants to hear them in a mature way. When you grumble in your problems, He thinks that you do not trust Him. God was preparing the Israelites for Canaan. He did not want complainers there. He did not want people who grumbled and complained in the new land. The wonderful blessings of the land of Canaan could not be achieved by people who had a problem with trusting God. There were many giants along the way, and one of the weapons they were going to use was faith. Faith is a strong assurance of things hoped for yet not seen.

Therefore, it was important for them to exercise that faith since they had already experienced the mighty and saving power of God. God delayed them and killed a whole generation of those who did not trust Him. He thoroughly cleaned off the complainers, until He was left with those who purely trusted Him.

Lamentations 3:26
It is good that one should hope and wait quietly for the salvation of the Lord.
NKJV

You might be going through a very tough crisis in your life. To avoid staying long in it, you should avoid complaining and develop a thankful heart all the time.

1 Corinthians 10:9-13
Nor let us tempt Christ, as some of them also tempted, and were destroyed by serpents;
10 nor complain, as some of them also complained, and were destroyed by the destroyer.
11 Now all these things happened to them as examples, and they were written for our Admonition, upon which the ends of the ages have come.
12 Therefore let him who thinks he stands take heed lest he fall.
13 No temptation has overtaken you except such as is common to man; but God is faithful, Who will not allow you to be tempted beyond what you are able, but with the temptation will Also make the way of escape, that you may be able to bear it.
NKJV

The other thing that God wanted them to destroy was the idols that they had worshipped in Egypt.
Exodus 20:3-5
Thou shalt have no other gods before me.
4 Thou shalt not make unto thee any graven image, or any likeness of anything that is in
Heaven above, or that is in the earth beneath, or that is in the water under the earth:
5 Thou shalt not bow down thyself to them, nor serve them: for I the Lord thy God am a Jealous God, visiting the iniquity of the fathers upon the children unto the third and fourth generation of them that hate me;
KJV

God does not want us mixing Him with other things. At times when we are listening to worldly evil music, we say, "It is alright", and go on listening even when the conscience is shouting loud in discomfort. I heard a story of a teenager once who was so hooked to pornography. When he was asked why he loves it so much he said he was learning the art side of honeymoon. This was clearly wrong but his excuses justified the fact that human beings always enjoy doing what is wrong in the eyes of God.

Grace Muigai

4.
SUFFERING THAT PRODUCES CHARACTER

I love listening to Prophet Uebert Angel's teaching on 'Dokime'. It really builds me up. 'Dokime' means 'approved character; also 'experience'; the quality of being approved as a result of test and trials. It is the character that is produced because of having fought tough battles and won. He says that Jesus was able to perform miracles because He underwent through so much suffering, despised and ashamed yet He endured all through to the cross. He even rose again after he was killed. He became a hero and it is for that reason that no demon stands His Name. For one to use His name and it works for you, you have to identify with that name. By that victory, what was developed is called character. Demons do not go just because of the name Jesus but because of the character behind the name Jesus. Ask those our brothers who are called Jesus today and tell me whether they can perform any of those single miracles like Jesus performed.

Character produces hope. Hope by itself will never give people victory. Many people have hoped for things and yet have never realized those hopes because they never moved into the realm of faith. Faith is the victory that causes people to overcome the world, yet it will not work without hope. Just as a thermostat activates the power unit on an air conditioner, so hope is what activates our faith. Faith only produces what we hope for, therefore being the first towards faith. The word 'hope' means 'a desire accompanied by confident expectation'. So, desiring the things of God with some expectation of obtaining them is the first step in walking in faith. When this hope is present, then faith begins to bring the desired thing into manifestation. If a delay is encountered, patience completes the work. Paul was saying that experience 'Dokime' worketh hope and is developed through tribulations.

Jesus himself went through great tribulations with a hope of overcoming the enemy. All this trials and tribulations, he went through patiently looking forward to what God had promised.

That is why all demons and powers must bow at the Name of Jesus; at the character of Jesus. The reason why demons go is they look at the character of the person sending them away. Somebody with a great character, or experience, demons cannot withstand such. That is why the sons of Sceva (Acts19:11-20) could not drive away those demons that they were trying to deliver.

One thing that he says is that God allows terrible problems to come to His great ministers so that they can operate on a higher level than all others. When great prophets and pastors undergo persecution coupled with insults and rejection, they in turn receive great anointing that makes them perform great miracles. According to him, great fire is deposited in them when they are suffering. Their performance is not based by how much they fast or pray but by how much they suffer for the sake of Christ.

Romans 8:28-30
And we know that all things work together for good to those who love God, to those who are
The called according to His purpose.
29 for whom He foreknew, He also predestined to be conformed to the image of His Son, that
He might be the firstborn among many brethren.
30 Moreover whom He predestined, these He also called; whom He called, these He also
Justified; and whom He justified, these He also glorified.
NKJV

The key thing in this verse is that of calling. God does not call everybody to do His work. He calls a few individuals to train them for His service. A people that

He calls must be a people that love Him. That is normally the first qualification. The bible says that 'for God so loved the world that He gave His only begotten son, that whosoever believeth in Him shall not perish but have eternal life.' He started by loving us. Those that respond to His love and embrace it become qualified. There are those who hear the message of love but do not want anything to do with it.

There are even some who either by choice or out of choice also move away further from His love. The story of the prodigal son has many teachings to offer unto us concerning how we should respond in His love. He exercised his power of choice and demanded his portion of wealth that was his by the virtue of inheritance. However, when he went and squandered all of it, he realized that his father would still offer solace even if he felt he did not deserve it. On going back, the father opened wide his arms and welcomed him back home, thus he responded to his father's love well. Would that compare to us? When we get back to God, we should receive the message of Christ's love, take it and cultivate it in their hearts. We should hunger and pant for it like the biblical deer in psalms 42:1

Psalms 42:1-2
As the deer pants for the water brooks, so pants my soul for You, O God.
2 My soul thirsts for God, for the living God. When shall I come and appear before God?
NKJV

Our desire and delight is in the law of the Lord. We should meditate on it day and night.
Psalms 1:2
But his delight is in the law of the Lord, and in His law he meditates day and night.
NKJV

This love is the prerequisite for God's call. From that point, the bible tells us that He calls us according to His purpose. Our God is full of purposes. Another word for purposes is 'objectives' or 'aims'. Each one of us is called according to His objective. That means, he already knows our purposes before He call us. When He called Jeremiah, He told him that He knew him before he was formed in his mother's womb.

Jeremiah 1:4-5
4 Then the word of the Lord came to me, saying:
5 "Before I formed you in the womb I knew you; before you were born I sanctified you; I Ordained you a prophet to the nations."
NKJV

He knew which male and female must come together to birth Jeremiah. That is how our God knows us. None of us is an accident. He has the reason why each and every one of us was formed in our mother's wombs. It is important for us to believe that we are fearfully and wonderfully made because we have been made for a purpose. So, Jeremiah was created with an objective of becoming a prophet who would prophesy to Israel. My spiritual father Prophet Shepherd Bushiri always puts it this way, Nine months in my mother's womb, just to prophesy!

Moses was created with an objective of becoming a deliverer. He would deliver the Israelites from the bondage of Egypt. Each one of us has a purpose in life. We should all know our purposes for which we were created. Some are preachers by calling, others are deliverers, others to treat the wounded are either physically, spiritually and even emotionally.

The next thing that happens is when they are also predestined to be conformed to the likeness of His son, that he might be the first-born among many brethren. Predestined means we are already decided for or planned for by God. That means that God knows the end of someone long way before he or she has started to exist. He told Jeremiah that He knew him before he was formed in his mother's womb. He had been sanctified before he had been born. To sanctify is to set apart or to declare holy; to purify and to authorize to be revered. All these had been done before Jeremiah had been born.

Then, interestingly, predestined to be conformed to the likeness of His Son. To conform is to make something to be similar to or the same as something and here is be like Jesus. Jesus underwent a lot of suffering before He was glorified. The same Jesus spoke the Word of God without fear or favor. Jesus had a lot of compassion on the poor and the sick and everywhere He went, he touched and blessed them. He made a difference in their lives. The bible says that,

Matthew 28:19-20
Go therefore and make disciples of all the nations, baptizing them in the name of the Father And of the Son and of the Holy Spirit,
20 teaching them to observe all things that I have commanded you; and lo, I am with you Always, even to the end of the age." Amen.
NKJV

John 1:50
Jesus answered and said to him, "Because I said to you, 'I saw you under the fig tree,' do you Believe? You will see greater things than these." NKJV

Ideally, God's plan is that, whomever He calls to go through all what Jesus went through and do the works like those of Jesus. One may not really die on the cross as Jesus did. That was a onetime salvation plan. However, real Christians may not escape hard times and persecutions. Those that have been called are also doing greater works as Jesus did and that is what is meant by conforming to the likeness of His Son. Therefore, Jesus becomes the first-born among many brothers. How many of us would have the faith of Jesus? For instance, Jesus was followed by a multitude of more than three thousand people and was able to feed them with only two fish and five loaves of bread! In other instances, he healed, raised the dead and did many other miraculous things. That is how God is conforming us to be like His Son. Therefore, whom that He predestinated, He also called and whom He called, He justified. To justify is to demonstrate or prove to be just.

Romans 3:24-26
Being justified freely by His grace through the redemption that is in Christ Jesus,
25 whom God set forth as a propitiation by His blood, through faith, to demonstrate His righteousness, because in His forbearance God had passed over the sins that were previously committed,
26 to demonstrate at the present time His righteousness, that He might be just and the justifier of the one who has faith in Jesus.

Romans 3:28
Therefore we conclude that a man is justified by faith apart from the deeds of the law.
NKJV

Romans 5:1-5
Therefore, having been justified by faith, we have peace with God through our Lord Jesus Christ,
2 through whom also we have access by faith into this grace in which we stand, and rejoice in hope of the glory of God.
3 And not only that, but we also glory in tribulations, knowing that tribulation produces perseverance;

*4 and perseverance, character; and character, hope.
5 Now hope does not disappoint, because the love of God has been poured out in our hearts by the Holy Spirit who was given to us.
NKJV*

*Romans 5:9
Much more then, having now been justified by His blood, we shall be saved from wrath through Him
NKJV*

*1 Corinthians 6:11
And such were some of you. But you were washed, but you were sanctified, but you were justified in the name of the Lord Jesus and by the Spirit of our God.
NKJV*

*Titus 3:7
that having been justified by His grace we should become heirs according to the hope of eternal life. NKJV*

All the scriptures above are teaching us how justification happens. The blood of Jesus justifies us. Once we are washed by it, then we can be counted among the saints and God can entrust to us the most treasured secrets. We are also justified through faith for the reason that when we were washed by the blood, it's the faith that made us take that bold step. Then by the grace of God we are also justified. Grace is the amazing favor or the kindness that God shows toward the human race. That also becomes our reason of justification. I could be a worthless sinner who after receiving Christ, can access all levels of grace because of justification. Think of Saul of Tarsus. God had purposed that He would call him to serve Him that was why He waited until the opportune time to call him. God was not worried by the many times that he went persecuting the Christians. He actually needed that exposure to make him more forceful in his service for God. Do you wonder why sometimes God calls and saves some fearful criminals and thugs who just deserved to be hanged in the face of the law? I have sometimes become amazed at God when He saves such people but it is only because he has to train us to be the best instrument.

That shows that God has already predestined his case and his purpose must be fulfilled. If God has called you, it is important to find out the purpose for your call. Whom He called, them were also justified. To justify is to have a good reason for doing something. One lady was rushed to a hospital one evening and was diagnosed with a problem of diabetes. She had not been sick before and even when doctors examined her, first of all they cancelled the fact that diabetes was in their family as history of the family proved it. Further examination proved that for her to be diabetic, was a mystery as all other facts stated differently. This lady one time testified, in a big conference that God was calling her to serve Him as she prayed and encouraged the diabetics. She later got healed completely and to date has no trace of diabetes in her.

This explains why God had a reason of allowing her to suffer from the same. She was being trained in the hard way for that service.

Why do we sometimes seem to be all of a sudden undergoing tough crisis in our lives. It is not because we have sinned and that God is punishing us for our sins. At times we are only being trained for His service. I know of a divorcee who later got together with his spouse, and was later used by God to heal marriages in crisis. You may also be undergoing financial strains but the sole reason is for you to be trained how to be a good manager of finances.

A good manager is refined through fire. A good marriage counselor is first taken through fire so as know what to tell others who have problems in their marriages. Think of a drug addict too who later tries to help others leave the problem of drugs.

Whom that He justified, He also glorified. It is true that after going through those moments of pain and frustration, a time comes and all pain ceases. God places us in a place of wealth. Some of the greatest preachers and ministers that we have today are people who went through a lot of pain and rejection in the past. I have from time to time listened to the great Prophet T. B Joshua of Nigeria as he keeps recounting the many times he underwent rejection from the very people that now adore him. After those times were over, tides came and changed the whole history concerning them. He also says, 'if you are born again, your pain will prepare you for extra-ordinary service.'

Consider the case of Jacob who labored in His uncle Laban's place for twenty one years but after that He went out a rich man with lots of cattle and two wives! Think of Joseph who was so much hated by his brothers that they even sold him to some merchants. Joseph knew and understood the purpose of it all, and waited patiently. When his time came he was glorified and become a vice pharaoh.

Glory is high fame and honor won by great achievements. It is beauty and splendor and also a special cause for pride and respect. Joseph was highly honored by the king and also his family. The very family that caused him misery and rejection turned to be the ones who bowed before him. He received glory from all corners of republic. The bible says that God will make your enemies to love you. That is what happened to Joseph. When you are in the process of being trained, it is important to endure to the end for in due course you will be glorified.

When, one is suffering, he is actually being modeled into God's best. If one is a great complainer, he is trained not to complain but to give praise. When the Israelites were in the wilderness, they complained so much and God actually wiped out a whole generation of those who complained. The next generation learnt to be careful with their mouths. They learnt the importance of giving praises which caused God to deliver them and bring them to the land of Canaan. It is only in pain when one learns the godly character. The reason why Job, a good man in the land underwent pain and misery is because God wanted Him to learn that God could allow anything to befall anyone.

The story of Job tells us how the devil went to request God to permit him to destroy him after accusing him. God allowed it to happen. Everything from Job was taken, including his children and all his wealth. Job did not sin against God by complaining but he only hoped strongly that God who had provided knew the reason for everything. He hoped that after losing all what he had, that God would only grant him everlasting life and rest without problems. Nevertheless, when God finally appeared after much suffering in great patience, he came to surrender to the fact that God was the Almighty and did what He saw right.

Job 42:1-6.
Then Job said to the Lord, I know you can do all things, and that no thought or purpose of Yours can be restrained or thwarted. (You said to me) Who is this that darkens and obscures counsel (by words) without knowledge? Therefore (I now see) I have (rashly) uttered what I did not understand, things too wonderful for me, which I did not know. (I had virtually said to You what You have said to me) hear , I beseech You, and I will speak; I will demand of You, and You declare to me. I had heard of

You (only) by the hearing of the ear, but now my (spiritual) eyes see You. Therefore I loathe (my words) and abhor myself and repent in dust and ashes. Amplified bible

God told Jeremiah to arise and go to the potter's house. He was to see how the potter mars clay in his hand and makes a pot according to his desire. God continued to tell him,

"at what instant I shall speak concerning a nation and concerning a kingdom, to pluck up, and to pull down, and to destroy it' Jer. 18:7

He alone determines the extent to which God mars someone. Yet, when one is being remolded, suffers pain and anguish until his time has come to be build up again.

Jer. 30:24. *The fierce anger of the LORD shall not return, until he have done [it], and until he have performed the intents of his heart: in the latter days ye shall consider it.* It is therefore important to be positive when we are suffering and seek God about it. God will always let us know why we are suffering and learn the character that God wants to instill in us.

My Journey Through a Wilderness

5.
FRIENDS DURING THE WILDERNESS

I have been in many types of wilderness and one that was the most terrible was a financial wilderness. My finances dwindled and I was like the proverbial ant that works hard but with nothing to show for it. I had many unpaid debts and bank loans. My friends disappeared from me and I really suffered even psychologically. Many people gossiped against me and would not want anything to do with me. It was such a terrible time for me. However, God finally came and set me free and all those who terrorized me in my time of problems became ashamed. Nevertheless, I had a brother in law who really stood with me even at that time when I was really down. He spoke to me and encouraged me along the way. He even assisted me with his own money and sustained me all along. I will also remained indebted to my two spiritual moms who also remained very close to me checking constantly how I was doing and chipping in here and there. By that time, my husband had travelled outside the country so I had no one to lean on at all. God provided this dear brother to me to lean on at that time. That was when I learnt the true meaning of friendship.

When you are suffering, it is possible to lose all friends that you have, as many will accuse and point their fingers at you. There are some, who come close to you with hidden motives. Take time to know the real and true friends. Some will come close to you because they want to show you where you failed and criticize you. Others will come close to you to give you encouragement and pray with you. These types of friends are very few.

Your friends really matter when you are in trials. The choice of friends can determine your direction and success. Your friends can influence you. When you are in the wilderness, you are very weak, disturbed and you need to lean on somebody for your emotional support.

Job had three friends who supported him very much. Even though whatever they advised Job, God did not accept it, they also played a big role in misleading him. This annoyed God so much until he commanded them to repent. Their repentance caused Job's turn around and he was delivered from his captivity.

Job 42:7. *And it was [so], that after the LORD had spoken these words unto Job, the LORD said to Eliphaz the Temanite, My wrath is kindled against thee, and against thy two friends: for ye have not spoken of me [the thing that is] right, as my servant Job [hath].*

8. Therefore take unto you now seven bullocks and seven rams, and go to my servant Job, and offer up for yourselves a burnt offering; and my servant Job shall pray for you: for him will I accept: lest I deal with you [after your] folly, in that ye have not spoken of me [the thing which is] right, like my servant Job.
9. So Eliphaz the Temanite and Bildad the Shuhite [and] Zophar the Naamathite went, and did according as the LORD commanded them: the LORD also accepted Job.
10. And the LORD turned the captivity of Job, when he prayed for his friends: also the LORD gave Job twice as much as he had before.
11. Then came there unto him all his brethren, and all his sisters, and all they that had been of his acquaintance before, and did eat bread with him in his house: and they bemoaned him, and comforted him over all the evil that the LORD had brought upon him: every man also gave him a piece of money, and every one an earring of gold.
12. So the LORD blessed the latter end of Job more than his beginning: for he had fourteen thousand sheep, and six thousand camels, and a thousand yoke of oxen, and a thousand she asses.
13. He had also seven sons and three daughters.
14. And he called the name of the first, Jemima; and the name of the second, Kezia; and the name of the third, Kerenhappuch.
15. And in all the land were no women found [so] fair as the daughters of Job: and their father gave them inheritance among their brethren.
16. After this lived Job an hundred and forty years, and saw his sons, and his sons' sons, [even] four generations.

17. So Job died, [being] old and full of days.

A friend who does not recognize the presence of God in your problems is not worth it. One who criticizes you in your problems should well be dropped. A friend can easily mislead you if you are not careful: Mostly, the kind of a friend you should have when you are having problems is one who plays the role of a mentor. A mentor helps breath life and actions into your intentions, transforming them into concrete goals and then providing you with the appropriate information and motivation to town your goals into glorious reality, as Mumbi Mbugua puts it in his book 'your dream is calling you'. When one is in the wilderness, it is usually because, he/she has agreed within the self that, that is not the proper place to stay. Therefore, it is because one has started to fight with the present circumstances and right in his mind, he/she can see what they want to become. Let me simplify it. You are living in poverty and that does not please you. You start imagining that, if God who is the owner of the universe is your God and you even claim to have a personal relationship with Him, then why is it that you are not able to tap His riches and direct them towards your life and you remain poor. Therefore, as you start calculating how you must stop being poor and become rich, you come face to face with harsh realities that actually throw you off balance. That is when you realize that you are in the wilderness. So, the kind of a friend, in the one who has probably gone through that kind of a problem and has succeeded. This person should also be very willing to lay down all what he/she has for the sake of the information and emotional support that you need. In addition, that this person will be in a position to walk with you on a daily basis offering you guidance, praying with you, offering you a shoulder to cry on when things are unbearable and just being there for you. Mentors are usually very eager to help. I quote again what Mbugua Mumbi says that if you are holding a candle in a dark room and you light another one, the room becomes more lighted. A mentor can only realize his or her success by helping others achieve what they themselves have achieved. No wonder, even a bride and a bridegroom also gets a best couple they think have achieved in their marriage. One that also has some experience in what marriage is all about and can share their experiences with them.

Therefore, it is not everybody who comes to laugh with you or to spend time with you should be your friend but one who can help finds solutions in what you are going through at that moment.

Prov.17:17 say that a friend is always loyal, and a brother is born to help in time of need.
The greatest evidence of genuine friendship is loyalty – being available to help in times of distress or personal struggle. Too many people are fair-weather friends. They stick around when the friendship helps them and leave when they are not getting anything out of the relationship. Think of your friends and assess your

loyalty to them. Be the kind of true friend the Bible encourages.

Loving your enemies

In most cases, enemies are the key factors of one's downfall. An enemy is a person who strongly dislikes or wants to injure or attack somebody. Surprisingly, an enemy is one person who is usually on a mission. The missions could be several and may include stealing your peace, harassing you and taunting your name. He is happy when you are discouraged and is satisfied with your downfall. He works very hard to see you are uncomfortable. An enemy could also be a disease, hunger, famine, drought persistence etc. all this come to take your peace.

When Joseph dreamt the dreams concerning his brothers bowing before him, they become jealous and did not receive the message well. They planned to kill him. One of the brothers saved the situation and convinced the others not to kill Joseph but sell him to some merchants.

Joseph -- Genesis 39:20-23
Joseph's master took him and put him in prison, the place where the king's prisoners were confined. But while Joseph was there in the prison, the Lord was with him; he showed him kindness and granted him favor in the eyes of the prison warden. So the warden put Joseph in charge of all those held in the prison, and he was made responsible for all that was done there. The warden paid no attention

to anything under Joseph's care, because the Lord was with Joseph and gave him success in whatever he did.

God was going to use Joseph to administer to the entire nation of Egypt. First, it was necessary for Joseph to learn gifts of administration. What did God do? He threw Joseph in prison. How discouraging this must have been for Joseph. He was there at least two years and maybe more. He could have become despondent and given up all hope. Instead, he tried to do a good job. Little did he know what God had in store for him. Barnes writes, "An uncomplaining patience and an unhesitating hopefulness kept the breast of Joseph in calm tranquility. There is a God above, and that God is with him. His soul swerves not from this feeling."

It is because Joseph was in the prison that the cupbearer would later remember him to Pharaoh. It is because Joseph was in prison that he learned the skills to be able to administer the grain storage for the king. It was because Joseph was in prison that he was able to spare his family from the famine. You may feel like you are in a prison, either trapped in a situation or relationship, or you may feel like you are in an emotional prison. Remember, that God used that time in prison so that Joseph could learn the skills he needed to minister to a nation and to his family! Perhaps God is using your prison too.

The purpose of the enemy

An enemy is in most cases is used by God to catapult you to your success. When he works for your fall, God uses take that to take you to your destiny. One should not hate the enemy. When somebody hurts you intentionally and wishes you bad in life, the only thing you can do is to love him. When you do that, it is as if you are placing coals of fire on his head. The bible says that we should love our enemies. It is only by the grace of God one can love him but God assures us of the ability to love them when we surrender our will completely to Him.

In most cases, an enemy is one who will cause one to be in the wilderness. He causes one to suffer mental and physical anguish. It is good to trust in God especially when the enemy is oppressing one. There is success and victory over the enemy when you trust in God.

Let us consider the case of Mordecai and Esther. Their great enemy was Haman. Haman would have done anything to see to the execution of the Jews. Mordecai and Esther were also Jews and this greatly shocked them. They planned to pray and fast. In fact, Mordecai tore his clothes and put on sackcloth and ashes and went through the city wailing with a loud and bitter cry. There was great mourning among the Jews with fasting, weeping, and lamenting. Haman would have wanted the Jews including Mordecai to die because he had realized that the king loved them. When God loves you, the enemy ignites hatred against you. The devil sends special demons to attack you so that you do not realize your blessing.

When the king realized that Haman indeed planned the execution of Jews, he made him to die in the very gallows that he had prepared for Mordecai. Do you not find that perplexing? When the enemy plans your fall, God in His mighty power changes it the other way round and you become the winner. Joseph did not become the slave that his brothers intended. He indeed went through a very tough process to become a loved one of God. Finally he did become a vice Pharaoh and helped his own brothers when problems arose. If an enemy is used this way by God to take you to your destiny, would you have any reasons of hating them? Is it possible to see him in the eyes of a friend but disguised to appear like an enemy?

When you dislike or hate your enemy, you are telling God that you are not ready for your promotion. Jesus insisted one time that we must love our enemies. He knew it was easy to love our friends and so did not have any problem with that. Read Luke 6: 27 and see what it says.

'Love your enemies and do well to those who hate you. Now, what credit is that to you if you only love those who love you as verse 32-34 says. *Love your enemies, do well and lend expecting nothing in return. Your reward will be great and you will be children of the Most High.*

It requires the grace of God for one to love someone who offended her or him deeply. The word of God assures us that everything is possible to him who believes. If you are willing and obedient, you shall eat the good of the land.

Joseph forgave his brothers for selling him to the Ishmaelite merchants. It is important for us to realize how enemies are our stepping-stones to our benefits and blessings.

6.
WHAT TO PRAY FOR DURING WILDERNESS

2 Corinthians 12: 8-10

For this thing I besought the Lord thrice, that it might depart from me.
9. And he said unto me, My grace is sufficient for thee: for my strength is made perfect in weakness. Most gladly therefore will I rather glory in my infirmities, that the power of Christ may rest upon me.
10. Therefore I take pleasure in infirmities, in reproaches, in necessities, in persecutions, in distresses for Christ's sake: for when I am weak, then am I strong.

The apostle gives an account of the method God took to keep him humble, and to prevent his being lifted up above measure on account of the visions and revelations he had. We are not told what this thorn in the flesh was, whether some great trouble, or some great temptation. But God often brings this good out of evil that the reproaches of our enemies help to hide pride from us. If God loves us, He will keep us from being excited above measure and spiritual burdens are ordered to cure spiritual pride. This thorn in the flesh is said to be a messenger of Satan which he sent for evil, but God designed it, and overruled it for good. Prayer is an ointment for every soul, remedy for every malady, and when we are afflicted, with thorns in the flesh, we should give ourselves to prayer. If an answer be not given to the first prayer nor to the second, we are to continue praying. Troubles are sent to teach us to pray and are continued to teach us to continue instant in prayer. Though God accepts the prayer of faith, yet He does not always give what Paul asked for; as He sometimes grants in wrath, so He sometimes deny in love. When God does not take away our troubles and temptations, yet if He gives grace enough for us, we have no reason to complain.

<u>Pray for grace</u>

Grace signifies the good will of God towards us, and that is enough to enlighten and enliven us, sufficient to strengthen and comfort in all afflictions and distresses. His strength is made perfect in our weakness.
Thus His grace is manifested and magnified. When we are weak in ourselves, then we go to Christ, receive strength from Him, and enjoy most of the supplies of Divine strength and grace.

You agree with me that the hardest task one can perform in tough times is praying. There are many reasons for this. It could be because of discouragement that results from torments that one is undergoing it could also result from stress that occurs from not getting the desired results in time. One may also lack to pray because of lack of faith at that time, that feeling of being overwhelmed by circumstances. Therefore, for one to pray successfully in hard times, one has to have a very strong will that is accompanied by strong faith.

<u>Pray for faith</u>.

Faith comes from reading and trusting the word of God. The bible says that David encouraged himself in the Lord. 1Sam 30:6

1 Samuel 30

1. And it came to pass, when David and his men were come to Ziklag on the third day, that the Amalekites had invaded the south, and Ziklag, and smitten Ziklag, and burned it with fire;
2. And had taken the women captives, that [were] therein: they slew not any, either great or small, but carried [them] away, and went on their way.
3. So David and his men came to the city, and, behold, [it was] burned with fire; and their wives, and their sons, and their daughters, were taken captives.
4. Then David and the people that [were] with him lifted up their voice and wept, until they had no more power to weep.
5. And David's two wives were taken captives, Ahinoam the Jezreelitess, and Abigail the wife of Nabal the Carmelite.
6. And David was greatly distressed; for the people spake of stoning him, because the soul of all the people was grieved, every man for his sons and for his daughters: but David encouraged himself in the LORD his God.

David is a perfect example of what anyone of us could go through when the enemy has been released. Amalekites had had a chance to destroy David and they thoroughly did it.

David and his men had left the town and then his foes got in from the southern side. They burnt it down and carried those women, sons and daughters into captivity. When David and his men came back, they discovered what the enemy had done and the bible says that David and his people raised their voices unto God. Then these people started planning to stone David as they looked upon him as the occasion of their calamities. The same way as we are today, when we are in trouble, we fly into a rage against those who are in any way the occasion of our trouble, while we overlook the divine providence, and have not that regard to the operations of God's hand in it which would silence our passions and make us patient. Before this happened, they had greatly depended on David, but now they are so disappointed to an extent of threatening his life. This was a sore trial to the man after God's own heart. Instead of David despairing like the way many of us would, the word says that he encouraged himself in the Lord. In another version, it says he strengthened his faith in the Lord. Great faith must expect such severe exercises but it is observable that David was reduced to this extremity just before his accession to the throne.

Things are sometimes at the worst with the church and the men of God just before they begin to mend. So, David bore it in a very interesting way. Though he had more reason than any of them to lament it, he set his graces on work. He kept his spirit calm and sedate. He encouraged himself in the Lord his God, believed, and considered the power and providence of God, His justice and goodness, the method He commonly takes of bringing low and then raising up, His care of His people that serve Him and trust in Him. He also put in his mind about the particular promises He had made to him of bringing him safely to the throne; with this considerations he supported himself, not doubting that the present trouble would end well.

Note, those that have taken the Lord for their God may take encouragement from their relation to him in the worst of times. It is the duty and interest of all good people, whatever happens, to encourage themselves in God as their Lord and their God, assuring themselves that He can and will bring light out of darkness, peace out of trouble, and good out of evil, to all that love Him and are called according to His purpose,

Rom. 8:28. *And we know that all things work together for good to them that love God, to them who are the called according to [his] purpose*

It was David's practice, and he had the comfort of it. What time I am afraid, I will trust in thee. When he was at his wit's end he was not at his faith's end. 1John 1:1 says *that the word of God is God Himself.*
When one reads the word of God, one actually discovers the mind of God. When you believe that word of God, you actually profess it and that way faith is built. Faith is the assurance of things hoped for yet not seen. One of the examples of people living in faith is Abraham who was very sure that he would have a son despite the old age.
When one believes the word of God, heavens must see to it that it is accomplished. A hard issue will always

have an answer in the bible. The answer given in the bible will not just work in the life of a Christian until activated. Activation is what a believer must know otherwise results will just be redundant.

Hebrews 13:5-6 states that [Let your] conversation [be] without covetousness; [and be] content with such things as ye have: for he hath said, I will never leave thee, nor forsake thee. So that we may boldly say, The Lord [is] my helper, and I will not fear what man shall do unto me.

He says that we are healed, so that we may say we are healed boldly. Not just believing, but also saying boldly. We must claim for our blessings boldly! We are missing out because we are not aware that we must say it boldly! We perish because we lack wisdom! We must have an impartation of the Holy Spirit to gain knowledge cum wisdom. What is it that is your obstacle to your blessing? Take the word of God that directly talks about your problem and deal with it until you bring that mountain down. We often struggle with problems that result from our own hard heartedness and yet others from our own carelessness. Whichever it is that reflects us, we can plan to change the direction of the tide so that we connect with the blessings of God.

<u>Pray for the endurance in the process of long suffering.</u> One of the things that God trains someone during the wilderness is long suffering. In other words being slow to anger. One can never become victorious if he or she

is not able to forgive those who have wronged them. Release them and forgive. The Holy Spirit is able to help one to forgive and overcome all the hurts.

<u>Pray for mercy</u>

It is important to pray that God has mercy on you during the difficult times. It is a time of heart ache and pain. A season where nobody understands you. This is a time when one requires the mercy from God.

<u>Pray for truthfulness</u>

This is an aspect of facing the reality as to why you are in that problem. If you have your own ugly weaknesses, it is important to confront them and deal with them. Pray that God helps you to accept what you really are and pray also for change.

<u>Pray that you understand the origin of your problems.</u>
Our problems may originate from various sources. Attacks from demonic forces, witchcraft and generational curses just to name a few.

Let me talk a little about generational curses as I mentioned earlier. There are some signs that have come down to us from our ancestors, we know some, and others we are not even aware we have them.

I have a friend called Jim and was married to Kate. Their marriage suffered from so many setbacks until a pastor advised both of them to look back to where they came from. Kate's mother had been divorced two times and more surprisingly, her grandmother had led a divorced life until she died. The pastor prayed with them and helped them severe themselves from the past that was threatening to tear them also. It is important to deal with ourselves by looking at our past and dealing with it severely. It could be problems like bad tempers, poverty etc. John spoke words of encouragement one time and said that 'little children ....God, who has given us all things that pertain to life. He continues at a different point that says that the enemy has taken all what God has given us and so we must take it by force!

When you do not have peace, you must get a way of having it by necessary force that is living faith. Faith will help us emerge as winners in a midst of hostile prevailing circumstances.

Therefore, it is important to pray in faith. Ask in faith. Talk in faith. Produce faith and let faith be your environment. If you do not have faith, do things that will help you acquire it. Read magazines and Christian books, which have been authored by God-fearing people. Listen to music that builds faith. Attend Christian meetings and most of all, study the word of God concerning what you could be undergoing and watch how your faith soars. Speak words of faith to your problem and see it disappear.

The enemy does not like when we read on confess words of faith because that is when he is brought down. When we pray and grow in faith, we overcome every obstacle on the way and he begins to fear. As he crumbles down, your victory gains foundation and what you achieve is total breakthrough in your problem whatever it is. Nothing is impossible with God, and God cannot work where there is no faith. I have come across people who are good at waiting for their problems to solve themselves, yet are not doing something about them. They will say something like, but God knows what I am undergoing right now. Yes, He knows and so he is waiting for you to act on it and the earlier the better.

When faith gains roots in our lives, it is possible then to pray to God. As we pray, we are not informing God of something He does not know, but we are agreeing with Him on what he wants to do. When we fast, we are not coercing God to do it, we are actually getting in line with what He has always desired to do and so, it happens when we gain such an understanding. It is important to realize the power behind prayers. Our prayers will bring down even the strongest adversary. An important lesson about Jesus.

Luke 5:16
16. And he withdrew himself into the wilderness, and prayed.

In the previous verses, we understand that after Jesus had taught and healed the multitudes, he withdrew into the wilderness and prayed. The wilderness was not only the place of Jesus greatest test and temptation, but also the place for being refueled spiritually. It was there, in the wilderness, alone with God and His thoughts that he prayed to continue in the will of God. Luke emphasizes the prayer life of Jesus more than any other gospel writer.

He often withdrew in such a manner, which means that this was not a onetime event. The multitudes often came to hear him teach and be healed. He often met their needs, and afterwards, withdrew to spend time in prayer.

Those who are mature in their Christian faith know that wilderness time is refueling time. Much problems that are handled maturely only escalate ones faith. After much performance in field, mature people know that it is not party time and celebration. It is time to go back to square one and listen to God again. God also helps one to avoid pride by taking the person to some trouble so that the person will spend more time in prayer.

7.
PERFORMING OTHER DUTIES DURING THE WILDERNESS

It is important to keep yourself busy when you are in the wilderness. Important practical lessons are learnt that way. Mostly, this is in the line of your call. This is not to mean that other issues that arise and not in your line of call should not be attended to but should also be tackled as they come. Therefore, they are important as we know they also keep one busy. A lot of brokenness is experienced during the wilderness thereby causing one to do whatever the duty with a lot of concern and seriousness. I want us to consider the story of Joseph, how he found himself in prison and how he utilized his time in prison.

Gen.39:12-23 And she caught him by his garment, saying, Lie with me: and he left his garment in her hand, and fled, and got him out.
13. And it came to pass, when she saw that he had left his garment in her hand, and was fled forth,
14. That she called unto the men of her house, and spake unto them, saying, See, he hath brought in an Hebrew unto us to mock us; he came in unto me to lie with me, and I cried with a loud voice:
15. And it came to pass, when he heard that I lifted up my voice and cried, that he left his garment with me, and fled, and got him out.
16. And she laid up his garment by her, until his lord came home.
17. And she spake unto him according to these words, saying, The Hebrew servant, which thou hast brought unto us, came in unto me to mock me:
18. And it came to pass, as I lifted up my voice and cried, that he left his garment with me, and fled out.
19..And it came to pass, when his master heard the words of his wife, which she spake unto him, saying, After this manner did thy servant to me; that his wrath was kindled.
20. And Joseph's master took him, and put him into the prison, a place where the king's prisoners [were] bound: and he was there in the prison.

21. But the LORD was with Joseph, and shewed him mercy, and gave him favour in the sight of the keeper of the prison.
22. And the keeper of the prison committed to Joseph's hand all the prisoners that [were] in the prison; and whatsoever they did there; he was the doer [of it].
23. The keeper of the prison looked not to anything [that was] under his hand; because the LORD was with him, and [that] which he did, the LORD made [it] to prosper.

Joseph refused to sleep with the Pharaoh's wife and this infuriated her. She decided to twist the case and say it was Joseph who wanted to rape her instead thus put him in prison. When he got into prison, he did not watch others suffer without intervention. He utilized his time helping fellow prisoners. Consider this time that the butler of the king of Egypt and his they had dreams and the only person who was able to help them understand their fate was Joseph.

Genesis 40
1. And it came to pass after these things, [that] the butler of the king of Egypt and [his] baker had offended their lord the king of Egypt.
2. And Pharaoh was wroth against two [of] his officers, against the chief of the butlers, and against the chief of the bakers.
3. And he put them in ward in the house of the captain of the guard, into the prison, the place where Joseph [was] bound.

4. And the captain of the guard charged Joseph with them, and he served them: and they continued a season in ward.
5. And they dreamed a dream both of them, each man his dream in one night, each man according to the interpretation of his dream, the butler and the baker of the king of Egypt, which [were] bound in the prison.
6. And Joseph came in unto them in the morning, and looked upon them, and, behold, they [were] sad.
7. And he asked Pharaoh's officers that [were] with him in the ward of his lord's house, saying, Wherefore look ye [so] sadly today?
8. And they said unto him, We have dreamed a dream, and [there is] no interpreter of it. And Joseph said unto them, [Do] not interpretations [belong] to God? tell me [them], I pray you.
9. And the chief butler told his dream to Joseph, and said to him, In my dream, behold, a vine [was] before me;
10. And in the vine [were] three branches: and it [was] as though it budded, [and] her blossoms shot forth; and the clusters thereof brought forth ripe grapes:
11. And Pharaoh's cup [was] in my hand: and I took the grapes, and pressed them into Pharaoh's cup, and I gave the cup into Pharaoh's hand.
12. And Joseph said unto him, This [is] the interpretation of it: The three branches [are] three days:
13. Yet within three days shall Pharaoh lift up thine head, and restore thee unto thy place: and thou shalt deliver Pharaoh's cup into his hand, after the former manner when thou wast his butler.

14. But think on me when it shall be well with thee, and shew kindness, I pray thee, unto me, and make mention of me unto Pharaoh, and bring me out of this house:
15. For indeed I was stolen away out of the land of the Hebrews: and here also have I done nothing that they should put me into the dungeon.
16. When the chief baker saw that the interpretation was good, he said unto Joseph, I also [was] in my dream, and, behold, [I had] three white baskets on my head:
17. And in the uppermost basket [there was] of all manner of bake meats for Pharaoh; and the birds did eat them out of the basket upon my head.
18. And Joseph answered and said, This [is] the interpretation thereof: The three baskets [are] three days:
19. Yet within three days shall Pharaoh lift up thy head from off thee, and shall hang thee on a tree; and the birds shall eat thy flesh from off thee. 20. And it came to pass the third day, [which was] Pharaoh's birthday, that he made a feast unto all his servants: and he lifted up the head of the chief butler and of the chief baker among his servants.
21. And he restored the chief butler unto his butlership again; and he gave the cup into Pharaoh's hand:
22. But he hanged the chief baker: as Joseph had interpreted to them.
23. Yet did not the chief butler remember Joseph, but forgot him.

Joseph interpreted their dreams. Remember that Joseph was performing his duty in line with is call. This same talent is the one that gave him his promotion. He interpreted king Pharaoh's dreams and earned himself a ticket to his promotion. Note that this God had given him a talent of dreams since he was very young. He had dreamed that he was binding sheaves with his brothers in the field where his self sheaf arose causing all the other sheaves belonging to his brothers to bow down to his sheaf.

Read Gen 37.
This caused a lot of envy to his brothers hence selling him away. We learn a very important lesson here. We get into the wilderness when God is perfecting our talents. Therefore, it is important for one to open eyes wide and look for opportunities to work on. As we do that, we practice what we shall be doing when we get out of the wilderness.

When Joseph got out of the wilderness, he earned his promotion and became the vice-pharaoh. He became in-charge of the food stores in Egypt when the time of drought came. He was also given a wife. You can see what happened overnight. He was set over all the land of Egypt. Pharaoh took off his ring form his hand and put it on Joseph's hand and arrayed him in vestures or garments of fine linen, and put a gold chain about his neck. Pharaoh made him to ride in a chariot and celebrated. He become second in command and nobody would step in command without the permission of Joseph. Therefore, he became satisfied materially, emotionally, socially and God's blessings were upon him.

I want us to learn a very important lesson here. He was put in prison because he refused to sin with Pharaoh's wife. Should he have committed adultery with her, he would have been cut off from his destiny. Some of the sins that we fall into during the temptations actually stop us from getting to our own destiny. It is important to keep watch and refuse to sin. Let us see far, beyond the joy of one day and purpose to run away from sin. When we resist the devil, he skips off. When we remain faithful in our wilderness, God takes us to our destiny and we
rejoice.

Ps 30:11 *you have turned my mourning into dancing. You have put of my sackcloth, and girded me with*

8.
CHOOSING TO OVERCOME

One counselor once told us that life is a choice. Whatever we do in life is out of the choices we make. When one goes to shop for something i.e. clothes, out of the power of choice, one may choose to buy any color depending on what color pleases him or her. If you find blue better to pink then you go home with blue.

So then, when one is in wilderness again the power of choice directs him or her to their desired direction. Those who do not want to rest until success comes by like

Joseph will keep on waiting until tomorrow comes. Of course, these positive minded people do not give up and in their mentality, they only know of good things not yet achieved. They are able to wait and persevere knowing that circumstances means well for them.

James 1:2-4 records –
My brethren, count it all joy, when you fall into divers temptations, knowing this, that the trying of your faith works patience. But let patience be perfect work, that you may be perfect and entire, wanting nothing.
Positive minded people whose purpose and vision is the choice of victory can only accept this kind of a scripture. The writers of this gospel do not even talk of

one or two temptations. He talks of divers or various trials. A Christian will not rest even after facing one trial. Even before he experiences the results of one trial, others keep on coming throughout the entire life. One may face critical periods like losing a loved one, and before mourning is over, another calamity strikes like a loss of business. Such things may continue being experienced, and this is where James advises the believers to count it all joy.

When one faces such calamities, and psychologists and counselors come in, they try to help the individuals by offering substitutes. They try to help one by letting them be calm. They advise someone to cry, shout and accept the situation, which seems to work shortly. However, a Christian who understands it all goes an extra mile- that one of counting it all joy. They pray such a prayer like, I thank you Lord for the kind of trials I am going through now, for I know that everything works together for my good. I also know that when your time comes, you will replace it with dancing. Amen.

You realize that, only a person of great faith can pray that kind of a prayer because he knows the importance of suffering. Maybe you are already asking, what is the importance of suffering then. I answer you by directing you to verse 3 of the same scripture that says, knowing this, that the trying of your faith works your patience. How many of us today have what we call tangible patience in us. If you are undergoing marital stress today, and then you are secretly told that God will, intervene in your marriage after five or so years, would you be able to wait for that long period or would you throw your hands and look for solution elsewhere like divorce or being unfaithful? A very close friend of mine once shared a really touching story with me of how after she flew back to Kenya from Canada where she had gone to study she found her husband with another woman. She really got frustrated and all her efforts to drive the woman away bore no fruits. In her frustration, she packed her bags and was just about to leave her matrimonial home when she heard a loud clear voice telling her not to go. "I have changed your husband for good".

The voice said. She knew that God had spoken for this was not the first time she was experiencing this voice. She unpacked and decided to stay knowing too well that when God speaks, He means it. But would you believe it that it was not until five long years that she actually experienced some change in this man. In fact, he even became worse. He would openly talk to this other woman on phone and would plan for night outs in his wife's presence. My friend was patient enough only thanking God and declaring repeatedly that God had said it and He is not a man that He should lie. After the five long and painful years, Mr. James (not his real name), was apprehended by traffic police one evening by driving in a very high speed under the influence of alcohol. He was put in a police cell overnight without the knowledge of his wife at home.

This did not raise alarm to her as she was used to his night escapades. The following day, he was arraigned in court and that was when his wife came to learn of his situation. When she went to see him, she found him full of tears in his eyes and apologized repeatedly to her. It was at that point that he gave his life to God and vowed to change for better. It is now many years after that episode and he has never done those things he used to do to irritate his wife. He became what God had said.

****
****

What if you become bankrupt and you were told that you would stabilize financially after seven or thirteen years. Would you choose to struggle with a very mean income or would you commit suicide or do other bad things. Incidentally, are you aware that you could be going through some of the problems only that you are not aware of the appointed time when you will finally overcome? Do you still realize that as you wait for that time when you finally make a sign of relief that God is actually working patience in you? So, knowing that God is working a very import ant virtue of godliness, in your life would you choose to quit or go on?

James 1:17 tell us that every
good gift and every perfect gift is from above and comes down from the Father of lights with whom is no variableness, neither shadow of turning.

Let us submit ourselves to God who is the author a finisher of our faith. Other than patience and being positive mindedness, one other thing I encourage the believers to develop a culture of praise when they are undergoing tough times. Many people think it is optional to praise God especially in hard times. Some Christians only praise God when their circumstances are good and they have a reason to thank Him. The truth is that praising God is not an option. Praise has powerful effect on the believer, the devil, and on God.

It is our highest calling. In Deuteronomy, God pronounced *a curse on the children of Israel because of not serving God with gladness of the heart and abundance of all things* (28; 47). Even though we are not under the law, this verse tells us that God wants us to have joyful and thankful hearts. Jesus was joyful. *Heb 1; 9 tells us that praising God at all times is part of the normal Christian life;*

I want to explain how praise affects the believer. When we praise God, we are acknowledging that it is not our own effort that produces blessings and prosperity. In Deuteronomy chapters 7 and 8, the children of Israel are told to remember to thank God for the abundance they WILL receive. God, not their own effort, gave them wealth. Praise makes us humble.

Thanksgiving is also a way to abound in faith. When time we operate in a high degree of faith, praise is present.

In *Colossians 2;6-7 says, as ye have therefore received Christ Jesus the Lord, so walk ye in Him; rooted and built up in Him, and established in the faith, as ye have been taught, abounding therein with thanksgiving.*
When you believe God for something, and it is completed, praise is a natural response. What some people often neglect is that they can increase their faith with praise, and their answers will come more quickly.
By focusing on your problems instead of praising God, you become self centered and prideful. Praise forces you to get your attention on God and off your problems. Some people say that they are praying, but they are so focused on their problems that they are actually complaining. If you focus on the word of God, faith will come. How do you keep from focusing on the problem when you are in pain and have no money?

The most important thing you can do is to praise God. A negative, complaining attitude will not change overnight but beginning to praise God will start the transformation in the attitude. If you have always been negative, you must practice thinking on positive things. *Philippians 4:4 tell us to rejoice in the Lord always; and again, I say, rejoices.*

When we pray, we should begin with praise and end with praise. The Lord's Prayer gives us this example, and *Philippians 4:6-7 tells us to be careful for nothing, but in everything by prayer and supplication with thanksgiving let your requests be made known unto God.*

And the peace of God, which passes all understanding, shall keep your hearts and minds through Christ Jesus. When you pray with thanksgiving, the peace of God will keep your heart and mind.

Praise will build you spiritually and keep you from crumbling, 'for the joy of the Lord is your strength'.

Neh. 8:10   Then he said unto them, Go your way, eat the fat, and drink the sweet, and send portions unto them for whom nothing is prepared: for [this] day [is] holy unto our Lord: neither be ye sorry; for the joy of the LORD is your strength

The Apostle Paul was persecuted and suffered far more than most of us yet, he put it all in perspective in *2 Cor 4:17-18: 'for our light affliction, which is but for a moment, worketh for us a far more exceeding and eternal weight of glory: while we look not at the things which are seen; for the things which are seen are temporal: but the thing which are not seen are eternal.'* First, Paul said our affliction is just for a moment in the light of eternity. He looked into the spiritual realm. Praise will push you into the spiritual realm to see what God has done for you. Paul and Silas praised God in prison. The praise released the power of God and earthquake that delivered them from their captivity.

Praising God does not just affect us; it is a powerful weapon against the devil as well.

Psalms 8:2 says, out of the mouth of babes and suckling hast thou ordained strength because of thine enemies, that thou mightiest still the enemy and the avenger.

'In the book of Matthew 21:16, at the time of triumphal entry into Jerusalem, Jesus quotes from psalms 8. When he quoted this verse, he interchanged the words.' Perfected praise 'for ordained strength'. This is a tremendous revelation: praise is strength (Neh 8:10).

Some people are so involved in the spiritual warfare that their attention is on the devil more than God is. There is a place for fighting and resisting the devil, but focusing too much on the devil is not good. Praise is a powerful weapon against the devil that has no negative fallout. In 2chronicles 20, Jehoshaphat appointed singers to lead his army into battle with praise unto the Lord. When they went into the battle singing and praising God, the Lord set an ambush, and their enemies were defeated.

Why does praise defeat Satan? Because Satan's sin was jealousy of God. He is still driven by jealousy today.

Is. 14:13-14. For thou hast said in thine heart, I will ascend into heaven, I will exalt my throne above the stars of God: I will sit also upon the mount of the congregation, in the sides of the
north: I will ascend above the heights of the clouds; I will be like the most High.

Even if he cannot get people to worship him, his goal is to keep people from worshipping God. He seeks to draw attention away from God. When we worship God, we thwart Satan's plan.

We have learnt the power of starting a service with praise. Praise makes the devil flee and releases the anointing of God. Even the secular world knows the benefit of praise. The medical profession says that a person who is joyful is healthier than a person who is morbid and depressed. Praise stops a negative attitude. The most important reason to praise God is that it ministers unto Him. *Acts 13* describes the situation at the church in Antioch.

Verse 2 says, 'as they ministered unto the Lord and fasted, the Holy Ghost said, separate me Barnabas and Saul for the work where unto I have called them.'
This is an awesome statement. They ministered to the Lord. How do you minister to the Lord? We often think we serve God only by ministering to other people. This happened in Matt 8, with Peter's mother-in-law. She waited on them and did household duties. That is a ministry. However, in this instance in Acts, they were fasting, praying and ministering to the Lord. They were glorifying and worshipping God. That also is a ministry to the Lord.

The truth is that God desires ministry. God is complete and self-contained, but He wants us to love Him. Any person who loves has a need to show that love and a need to have that love returned. That is the reason for the creation of man in the first place. In *Rev. 4*, John saw a vision of what is happening in heaven. He saw 24 elders and 4 living creatures that do not cease praising God.

In vs. 11, the elder said, thou art worthy, o Lord, to receive glory and honor and power: for thou hast created all things, and for thy pleasure, they are and were created.
'This tells us that God's original and current purpose for creation is for His pleasure. God created us to be full of praise, joy and thanksgiving. He is blessed by His creation.

God longs to know us personally and intimately. There are hundreds of times in scripture that God solicits our praise.

Ps 100; 4 says that we should enter His gates with thanksgiving, and Into His courts with praise and bless His Name.

Service is not a substitute for a relationship with God. Our number 1 priority must be to love God personally. Praise is giving of you to God- an intimate communion with Him. It is a way to begin the love relationship with God.

By Him therefore, let us offer the sacrifice of praise to God continually, that is, the fruit of
our lips, giving thanks to His Name. Heb. 13:15

Grace Muigai

9.
MARCHING TO VICTORY

There is a song that I used to love so much when I was in High School that says;
The battle belongs to the Lord
In heavenly armor, we'll enter the land
The battle belongs to the Lord
No weapon that's fashioned against us shall stand
The battle belongs to the Lord

We sing glory and honor
Power and strength to the Lord (repeat)

The power of darkness comes in like a flood
The battle belongs to the Lord
He's raised up a standard, the power of His blood
The battle belongs to the Lord

We sing glory and honor
Power and strength to the Lord (repeat)

When your enemy presses in hard, do not fear
The battle belongs to the Lord
Take courage my friend, your redemption is near
The battle belongs to the Lord

The battle belongs to the Lord
The battle belongs to the Lord

We used to sing it with so much vigor as it really used to bless our souls. That is to say, if you are in a battle right now, you have to understand that it is not your

battle but the Lord's. If you are to succeed and win victoriously, the Lord has to be the One fighting the battle.
2 Chronicles 20: 1-29

*.	It came to pass after this also, [that] the children of Moab, and the children of Ammon, and*
with them [other] beside the Ammonites, came against Jehoshaphat to battle.
2. Then there came some that told Jehoshaphat, saying, There cometh a great multitude against thee
from beyond the sea on this side Syria; and, behold, they [be] in Hazazontamar, which [is] Engedi.
3. And Jehoshaphat feared, set himself to seek the LORD, and proclaimed a fast throughout all
Judah.
4. And Judah gathered themselves together, to ask [help] of the LORD: even out of all the cities of
Judah they came to seek the LORD.
5. and Jehoshaphat stood in the congregation of Judah and Jerusalem, in the house of the LORD,
before the new court,
6. and said, O LORD God of our fathers, [art] not thou God in heaven? And rules [not] thou over all
the kingdoms of the heathen? In addition, in thine hand [is there not] power and might, so that none is able to withstand thee?
7. [Art] not thou our God, [who] didst drive out the inhabitants of this land before thy people Israel, and gavest it to the seed of Abraham thy friend forever?

8. and they dwelt therein, and have built thee a sanctuary therein for thy name, saying,
9. If, [when] evil cometh upon us, [as] the sword, judgment, or pestilence, or famine, we stand before this house, and in thy presence, (for thy name [is] in this house,) and cry unto thee in our affliction, then thou wilt hear and help.
10. and now, behold, the children of Ammon and Moab and mount Seir, whom thou wouldest not let Israel invade, when they came out of the land of Egypt, but they turned from them, and destroyed them not;
11. Behold, [I say, how] they reward us, to come to cast us out of thy possession, which thou hast given us to inherit.
12. O our God, wilt thou not judge them? For we have no might against this great company that cometh against us; neither know we what to do: but our eyes [are] upon thee.
13. and all Judah stood before the LORD, with their little ones, their wives, and their children.
14. Then upon Jahaziel the son of Zechariah, the son of Benaiah, the son of Jeiel, the son of Mattaniah, a Levite of the sons of Asaph, came the Spirit of the LORD in the midst of the congregation;
15. and he said, Hearken ye, all Judah, and ye inhabitants of Jerusalem, and thou king Jehoshaphat, Thus saith the LORD unto you, be not afraid nor dismayed by reason of this great multitude; for the battle [is] not yours, but God's.

16. tomorrow go ye down against them: behold, they come up by the cliff of Ziz; and ye shall find them at the end of the brook, before the wilderness of Jeruel.
17. Ye shall not [need] to fight in this [battle]: set yourselves, stand ye [still], and see the salvation of the LORD with you, O Judah and Jerusalem: fear not, nor be dismayed; tomorrow go out against them: for the LORD [will be] with you.
18. And Jehoshaphat bowed his head with [his] face to the ground: and all Judah and the inhabitants of Jerusalem fell before the LORD, worshipping the LORD.
19. and the Levites, of the children of the Kohathites, and of the children of the Korhites, stood up to
praise the LORD God of Israel with a loud voice on high.
20. and they rose early in the morning, and went forth into the wilderness of Tekoa: and as they went forth, Jehoshaphat stood and said, Hear me, O Judah, and ye inhabitants of Jerusalem; Believe in the LORD your God, so shall ye be established; believe his prophets, so shall ye prosper.
21. and when he had consulted with the people, he appointed singers unto the LORD, and that should praise the beauty of holiness, as they went out before the army, and to say, Praise the LORD; for his mercy [endureth] forever.
22. and when they began to sing and to praise, the LORD set ambushments against the children of Ammon, Moab, and mount Seir, which were come against Judah; and they were smitten.
23. for the children of Ammon and Moab stood up against the inhabitants of mount Seir, utterly to slay and destroy

[them]: and when they had made an end of the inhabitants of Seir, every one helped to destroy another.
24. and when Judah came toward the watch tower in the wilderness, they looked unto the multitude, In addition, behold, they [were] dead bodies fallen to the earth, and none escaped.
25. and when Jehoshaphat and his people came to take away the spoil of them, they found among them in abundance both riches with the dead bodies, and precious jewels, which they stripped off for themselves, more than they could carry away: and they were three days in gathering of the spoil, it was so much.
26. and on the fourth day, they assembled themselves in the valley of Berachah; for there they blessed The LORD: Therefore, the name of the same place was called, the valley of Berachah, unto this day.
27. Then they returned, every man of Judah and Jerusalem, and Jehoshaphat in the forefront of them, to go again to Jerusalem with joy; for the LORD had made them to rejoice over their enemies.
28. And they came to Jerusalem with psalteries and harps and trumpets unto the house of the LORD.
29. And the fear of God was on all the kingdoms of [those] countries, when they had heard that the LORD fought against the enemies of Israel.
30. So the realm of Jehoshaphat was quiet: for his God gave him rest round about.

This story is one of many examples of stories where we see the Lord fighting for His people.

Judah gathered to seek help from the Lord; they even came from all the cities of Judah to seek the Lord.
Then Jehoshaphat stood in the assembly of Judah and Jerusalem, in the house of the Lord before the new court, and he said, 'O Lord, the God of our fathers, are you not God in the heavens? And are you not the ruler over all the kingdoms of the nations? Power and might are in your hand so that no one can stand against you." (Two Chr 20:4-6)

An alliance of Moab, Ammon and others had invaded Judah. It was a matter of mathematics; the enemy by far out-numbered the people of Judah. There seemed to be only one possible outcome; the defeat of Judah. Jumping up, Jehoshaphat stood in the temple and prayed. There was only one place to turn. Sometimes life is like that. In addition, with reference to death, and eternity, God is the only one who can make a difference!
The Lord responded through His prophet, Jahaziel. *"…and he said, "listen, all Judah and inhabitants of Jerusalem and King Jehoshaphat: thus says the Lord to you "do not fear or be dismayed because of this great multitude, for the battle is not yours but God's." (2 Chron. 20:15)*

Yes, here was a case where the battle had to be the Lord's, or it would be lost. However, that the battle was the Lord's did not mean that the people of Judah were to sit and do nothing. They were instructed:

you need not fight in this battle; station yourselves, stand and see the salvation of the Lord on your behalf, O Judah and Jerusalem." Do not fear or be dismayed; tomorrow go out to face them, for the Lord is with you." (2 Chron. 20:17).

They went out and faced their enemy, and the Lord gave them victory as they watched their enemy's alliance fall apart and the former allies attack one another. We can rely on the Lord's strong arm.

Isaiah 40:9-11
9. O Zion, that bringest good tidings, get thee up into the high mountain; O Jerusalem, that bringest good tidings, lift up thy voice with strength; lift [it] up, be not afraid; say unto the Cities of Judah, Behold your God!
10 Behold, the Lord GOD will come with strong [hand], and his arm shall rule for him: behold his reward [is] with him, and his work before him.
11 He shall feed his flock like a shepherd: he shall gather the lambs with his arm, and carry [them] in his bosom, [and] shall gently lead those that are with young
When we fully place our confidence in God. We can match to victory if we can have a God who has that kind of power. His power is directed by His love, and what His love motivated Him to give for us.

(John 3:16). For God so loved the world, that he gave his only begotten Son, that whosoever believeth in him should not perish, but have everlasting life.

Understand and comprehend with whom all things are possible. *(Matt 19:25-26). 25. When his disciples heard [it], they were exceedingly amazed, saying, who then can be saved? 26 But Jesus beheld [them], and said unto them, with men this is impossible; but with God all things are possible*

Recognize that He is a God who is able to know our needs even beyond what *we know ourselves!*

(Eph 3:14-21). 14. For this cause I bow my knees unto the Father of our Lord Jesus Christ, 15 of whom the whole family in heaven and earth is named, 16 That he would grant you, according to the riches of his glory, to be strengthened with might by his Spirit in the inner man; 17. That Christ may dwell in your hearts by faith; that ye, being rooted and grounded in love, 18. May be able to comprehend with all saints what [is] the breadth, and length, and depth, and height; 19. And to know the love of Christ, which passes knowledge, that ye might be filled with all the fullness of God. 20. Now unto him that is able to do exceeding abundantly above all that we ask or think, according to the power that worketh in us, 21. Unto him [be] glory in the church by Christ Jesus throughout all ages, world without end. Amen.

He is not limited by our lack of imagination, creativity, vision or power as we are.

Do you recall the ancient nation of Israel, after witnessing God's power in many ways; the ten plagues on their Egyptian masters, their deliverance at the Red Sea; how that nation still, tragically, lacked confidence in God's power as they stood on the brink of the promised land of Canaan (Num. 12-13)? God was able, but they were unwilling to believe. God would have given them whatever they needed to win the victory, if only they had believed.

That was then, now is now. We find ourselves in similar circumstances and that is not by accident. The Lord caused the account of Israel's failure of faith to be recorded and preserved so that we might learn not to do likewise; "now these things happened to them as an example, and they were written for our instructions, upon which the ends of the ages have come." (1Cor.10:11). *11. Now all these things happened unto them for ensamples: and they are written for our admonition, upon whom the ends of the world are come.*

God would have blessed them with whatever strength they would need. He wills us as well. We are yet in the wilderness, and God will bring us home if we have the trust and humility to submit to Him.

(1 Peter 5:6-7 .*Humble yourselves therefore under the mighty hand of God, that he*
May exalt you in due time: 7. casting all your care upon him; for he careth for you.

Grace Muigai

10.
RECEIVING THE GLORY

When I was employed in my first place of work, our Director was a Satanist and before we came to know what kind of a person she was, she had already done so much to destroy God's work. I had been assigned to be the Christian Union patron and she accused me of preaching too much. In fact, she even said that the students were praying too much instead of using that time to study. Therefore, she exempted me from that duty and placed another one who was not very fiery in spiritual matters. She did everything in her power to undo all what we had done to build the church. In turn, we started praying earnestly for God to intervene in His own way. God did not intervene as soon as we wanted it; instead, He took us through a slow and painful process of being ridiculed openly. God wanted to use her to purge our weaknesses and sins too so that when He eventually brings us up, He will destroy the evil at the same time. It was time for us to repent our wicked ways and turn to God totally. All this time, the enemy taunted at us but God in His graces cushioned us. That is what He eventually did. After such a long time, we started experiencing victory. God started causing shame upon her in public and her demeanor started to go down. In the meantime, what we had lost we started having it back until even those who had openly mocked us got ashamed of it. They confessed eventually that God was with us. We have a lot of joy now and that Director was thrown out. Today we have a God fearing Director and our glory is back. Praise God.

1 Sam 17:4-58
And there went out a champion out of the camp of the Philistines, named Goliath, of Gath, whose height [was] six cubits and a span.
5. And [he had] an helmet of brass upon his head, and he [was] armed with a coat of mail; and
the weight of the coat [was] five thousand shekels of brass.
6. And [he had] greaves of brass upon his legs, and a target of brass between his shoulders.
7. And the staff of his spear [was] like a weaver's beam; and his spears head [weighed] six hundred shekels of iron: and one bearing a shield went before him.

8. *And he stood and cried unto the armies of Israel, and said unto them, why are ye come out to set [your] battle in array? [am] not I a Philistine, and ye servants to Saul? choose you a man for you, and let him come down to me.*
9. *If he be able to fight with me, and to kill me, then will we be your servants: but if I prevail against him, and kill him, then shall ye be our servants, and serve us.*
10. *and the Philistine said, I defy the armies of Israel this day; give me a man, that we may fight together.*
11. *When Saul and all Israel heard those words of the Philistine, they were dismayed, and greatly afraid.*
12. *Now David [was] the son of that Ephrathite of Bethlehem, judah, whose name [was] Jesse; and he had eight sons: and the man went among men [for] an old man in the days of Saul.*
13. *And the three eldest sons of Jesse went [and] followed Saul to the battle: and the names of his three sons that went to the battle [were] Eliab the firstborn, and next unto him Abinadab, and the third Shammah.*
14. *And David [was] the youngest: and the three eldest followed Saul.*
15. *But David went and returned from Saul to feed his father's sheep at Bethlehem.*
16. *And the Philistine drew near morning and evening, and presented himself forty days.*
17. *And Jesse said unto David his son, Take now for thy brethren an ephah of this parched [corn], and these ten loaves, and run to the camp to thy brethren;*
18. *And carry these ten cheeses unto the captain of [their] thousand, and look how thy brethren fare, and take their pledge.*

19. Now Saul, and they, and all the men of Israel, [were] in the valley of Elah, fighting with the Philistines.

20. And David rose up early in the morning, and left the sheep with a keeper, and took, and went, as Jesse had commanded him; and he came to the trench, as the host was going forth to the fight, and shouted for the battle.

21. For Israel and the Philistines had put the battle in array, army against army.

22. And David left his carriage in the hand of the keeper of the carriage, and ran into the army, and came and saluted his brethren.

23. And as he talked with them, behold, there came up the champion, the Philistine of Gath, Goliath by name, out of the armies of the Philistines, and spake according to the same words: and David heard [them].

24. And all the men of Israel, when they saw the man, fled from him, and were sore afraid.

25. And the men of Israel said, Have ye seen this man that is come up? surely to defy Israel is
he come up: and it shall be, [that] the man who killeth him, the king will enrich him with great riches, and will give him his daughter, and make his father's house free in Israel.

26. And David spake to the men that stood by him, saying, What shall be done to the man that killeth this Philistine, and taketh away the reproach from Israel? for who [is] this uncircumcised Philistine, that he should defy the armies of the living God?

27. And the people answered him after this manner, saying, So shall it be done to the man that killeth him.

28. And Eliab his eldest brother heard when he spake unto the men; and Eliab's anger was kindled against David, and he said, Why camest thou down hither? and with whom hast thou left those few sheep in the wilderness? I know thy pride, and the naughtiness of thine heart; for thou art come down that thou mightiest see the battle.
29. And David said, What have I now done? [Is there] not a cause?
30. And he turned from him toward another and spake after the same manner: and the people answered him again after the former manner.
31. And when the words were heard which David spake, they rehearsed [them] before Saul: and he sent for him.
32. And David said to Saul, Let no man's heart fail because of him; thy servant will go and fight with this Philistine.
33. And Saul said to David, Thou art not able to go against this Philistine to fight with him: for thou [art but] a youth, and he a man of war from his youth.
34. And David said unto Saul, Thy servant kept his father's sheep, and there came a lion, and a bear, and took a lamb out of the flock:
35. And I went out after him, and smote him, and delivered [it] out of his mouth: and when he arose against me, I caught [him] by his beard, and smote him, and slew him.
36. Thy servant slew both the lion and the bear: and this uncircumcised Philistine shall be as
one of them, seeing he hath defied the armies of the living God.

37. David said moreover, The LORD that delivered me out of the paw of the lion, and out of the paw of the bear, he will deliver me out of the hand of this Philistine. And Saul said unto David, Go, and the LORD be with thee.
38. And Saul armed David with his armor, and he put an helmet of brass upon his head; also he armed him with a coat of mail.
39. And David girded his sword upon his armor and he assayed to go; for he had not proved [it]. And David said unto Saul, I cannot go with these; for I have not proved [them]. And David put them off him.
40. And he took his staff in his hand, and chose him five smooth stones out of the brook, and put them in a shepherd's bag which he had, even in scrip; and his sling [was] in his hand: and he drew near to the Philistine.
41. And the Philistine came on and drew near unto David; and the man that bare the shield [went] before him.
42. And when the Philistine looked about, and saw David, he disdained him: for he was [but] a youth, and ruddy, and of a fair countenance.
43. And the Philistine said unto David, [Am] I a dog that thou comest to me with sticks? And the Philistine cursed David by his gods.
44. And the Philistine said to David, Come to me, and I will give thy flesh unto the fowls of the air, and to the beasts of the field.
45. Then said David to the Philistine, Thou comest to me with a sword, and with a spear, and with a shield: but I come to thee in the name of the LORD of hosts, the God of the armies of Israel, whom thou hast defied.

46. *This day will the LORD deliver thee into mine hand; and I will smite thee, and take thine head from thee; and I will give the carcasses of the host of the Philistines this day unto the fowls of the air, and to the wild beasts of the earth; that all the earth may know that there is a God in Israel.*
47. *And all this assembly shall know that the LORD saveth not with sword and spear: for the*
battle [is] the LORD'S, and he will give you into our hands.
48. *And it came to pass, when the Philistine arose, and came and drew nigh to meet David, that David hasted, and ran toward the army to meet the Philistine.*
49. *And David put his hand in his bag, and took thence a stone, and slang [it], and smote the Philistine in his forehead that the stone sunk into his forehead; and he fell upon his face to the earth.*
50. *So David prevailed over the Philistine with a sling and with a stone, and smote the Philistine, and slew him; but [there was] no sword in the hand of David.*
51. *Therefore David ran, and stood upon the Philistine, and took his sword, and drew it out of the sheath thereof, and slew him, and cut off his head therewith. And when the Philistines saw their champion was dead, they fled.*
52. *And the men of Israel and of Judah arose, and shouted, and pursued the Philistines, until thou come to the valley, and to the gates of Ekron. And the wounded of the Philistines fell*
down by the way to Shaaraim, even unto Gath, and unto Ekron.
53. *And the children of Israel returned from chasing after the Philistines, and they spoiled their tents.*

54. And David took the head of the Philistine, and brought it to Jerusalem; but he put his armor in his tent.
55. And when Saul saw David go forth against the Philistine, he said unto Abner, the captain of the host, Abner, whose son [is] this youth? And Abner said, [As] thy soul liveth, O king, I cannot tell.
56. And the king said, Enquire thou whose son the stripling [is].
57. And as David returned from the slaughter of the Philistine, Abner took him, and brought him before Saul with the head of the Philistine in his hand.
58. And Saul said to him, Whose son [art] thou, [thou] young man? And David answered, I
[am] the son of thy servant Jesse the Bethlehemite.

Now Goliath over nine feet tall taunted Israel's soldiers and appeared invincible to them. Saul the tallest of the Israelites may have been especially worried because he was obviously the best match for Goliath. In God's eyes, however, Goliath was no different from anyone else. God was not worried of the size or the shape of the enemy. Your Goliath may appear so big in your eyes but God sees nothing.

Therefore, he continued shouting across to the Israelites, whether they needed a whole army to settle that. He offered himself to represent the philistines and challenged the Israelites to do the same. "If your man is able to kill me, then we will be your slaves. However, if I kill him you will be our slaves! He defied all the armies of armies of Israel and this caused terror and fear among the Israelites. This went on for forty days without one side attacking the other. They were camped an opposite sides of a valley with steep walls. Whoever would rush down the valley and up the steep cliffs would be at a disadvantage at the beginning of the battle and probably suffer great casualties. Each side was waiting for the other to attack first. David was sent by his father to take food to his brothers who were fighting. He left the sheep with another shepherd and left for the camp. When he arrived there, he left his things with the storekeeper and hurried to greet his brothers. As he exchanged greetings, Goliath the champion from Gath came out from the philistine ranks counting his challenge to the army of Israel.

As he looked at him taunting the Israelites and defying the name of the Almighty God, anger swelled inside him and started inquiring more about what the King had promised to anyone who killed this foe. There was a huge reward and one of his daughters. His whole family would be exempted from paying the taxes too! With this in mind, he remembered his experiences with wild animals in the wilderness and how he had killed each of them that attacked his father's sheep.

Saul tried to discourage him saying that he was only a small boy but that did not deter him from doing what his heart had decided. Goliath had the definite advantage against David from a human stand point, what Goliath did not realize was that in fighting David, he also had to fight God. The way each human being sees a thing makes all the difference. All the other Israelites saw a giant while David saw a mortal man defying Almighty God. He knew he would not be alone when he faced Goliath but God would fight with him. He looked at his situation from God's point of view viewing impossible situations from God's point of view helps us put giant problems in perspective.

Saul tried to stop him when he suggested about fighting the philistine. He told him to stop being ridiculous. His own brothers thought he was crazy when he offered himself to kill Goliath. Criticism could not stop David while the rest of the army stood around; he knew the importance of taking action. He did not see the reason of waiting when it was God who was fighting for Him. People may try to discourage you with negative comments or mockery but you should continue to do what you know is right because you will please God, whose opinion matters most.

He took his shepherd's bag and went to collect five smooth stones from a stream. He carried himself with a shepherd's staff and sling and started across to fight Goliath. What followed that was like drama before the eyes of all onlookers. Goliath walked towards him with a sneer, the shield bearer ahead of him. "Am I a dog that you come to me with a stick," Goliath roared. "I will give your flesh to the birds and wild animals". He yelled. David replied, "You come to me with a sword, spear and javelin but I come to you in the Name of the Lord Almighty, the God of armies of Israel whom you've defied. Today the Lord will conquer you, and I will kill you and cut off your head and will give the dead bodies of your men to the birds and wild animals and the whole world will know that there is a God in Israel. Everyone will know that the Lord does not need weapons to rescue his people. It is His battles not ours. The Lord will give you to us! Goliath moved closer to attack and David ran out to meet him. He took out a stone, hurled it from his sling, and hit the philistine in the forehead. The stone, sank in, Goliath stumbled and fell face download to the ground. He died and David used Goliath's sword to cut off his head. Then the philistines feared and ran when they saw that their champion had died. The Israelites actually slew so many and plundered the deserted philistine camp.

How many times has the enemy taunted you with insults that you cannot be able to overcome him? How many times has he laughed at your calamities and you have been tormented and intimidated as he has continually defied your God? You could change your way of seeing him and start looking at him in God's point of view. Draw your strength from what David did and you will surely overcome him.

David therefore took Goliath's head to Jerusalem and delivered it to Saul. All the promises that had been promised to anyone who would kill Goliath actually went to David. David moved and started staying in the palace. He became a friend to Jonathan —Saul son. After this, Saul made David a commander in his army, an appointment that was applauded by the fighting men and officers alike.

God is able to uplift all those who fight their enemies and succeed. They are given a special place of honor either at the church, in the government or the community. They receive the glory that is never received by all the other people. Dare fight your financial problems, marital problems or any other that you are going through light now and God will give you that special seat of honor. Amen.

My Journey Through a Wilderness

11.
REMAINING A WINNER

This is a true account of a dear friend who sometimes back invited me for a cupper of coffee to share with me. "I have known Sheila for close to thirty years," she started. "And I have never had a reason to believe that she had a weakness in handling finances especially that belonged to a third party." She went on. Sheila was a family friend and she was doing very well with her husband in business. They had a string of businesses in one of the major cities in this country.

Sheila's husband was quite a gentleman in every other aspect though he had this major weakness; he was very mean with money as the wife put it. When the wife wanted to finish putting up a floor of an institution she was building, the husband would not assist her financially.

The couple would develop their separate businesses without the involvement of each other.

"Finances are over and I don't know what to do," she told Shelmith. That was six years back. Shelmith was quite concerned but being financially incapacitated too, she did not know how else to help her friend Sheila. But as they were talking, a thought came to Sheila and told Shelmith.
"You are a good friend to my husband, aren't you?"

"Yes I am" Shelmith answered.
"Why don't you ask him for a loan on my behalf, then when my building is done and business has picked up, then I will give you back the money and give it to him."

Sheila went on. Shelmith would not have had any reason of refusing that request, as all she wanted was to help her friend out. Therefore, the following day Shelmith approached Mr. Jones and after exchanging a few pleasantries, she broached the subject.

"You have known my diabetic problem ever since and how last month I had a breakdown. You also know how my eyes got affected....."

"Yes I remember my wife telling me that your niece was leading you by your hand... you became partially blind..." Mr. Jones interjected.

"It was a sad state of affairs indeed," they continued.

"I have been fortunate enough to get a doctor specialist from S. Africa," she said. She went on to explain how she had been able to raise half the required amount and now she required from him the remaining half for her operation.

Mr. Jones was kind enough to loan her the amount she was asking for and happily went to meet his wife.

Sheila was more than excited and she embarked on finishing what she was building.

Her work went on very well and furnished the project in a span of three months. Unfortunately, her business did not pick as she expected and did not inform Shelmith about it. It would have been possible for her to apply for a loan from a bank since she had other sources of income but she did not do it.

Shelmith continued to wait for Sheila to respond but the response was not forthcoming. She decided to broach the subject for discussion and called Sheila.

"Shelmith I am grateful to you because you helped me when I was in need. However, I am not able to give you back that money but since it belongs to my husband, you may as well forget about it!" Sheila said.

"But that was not the agreement Sheila!" Shelmith almost shouted back to her.

"I know!" she said.

"For heaven's sake Sheila, what do you think your husband will take me for? We have been buddies for a long time; do you want to destroy our friendship because of a mere debt? Surely, it is my name that you are destroying Sheila! Shelmith said in an agitated tone.

"Okay, Shelmith! Give me time I will see what I can do." Said Sheila. After a short time, Shelmith had another thought.

"Sheila, I have another idea. Why don't we go to your husband, and I explain the situation to him in your presence so that I am vindicated and then I go my way?"

Sheila could not listen to that since she feared her husband very much and refused vehemently the suggestion.

They left each other and Shelmith went her way. Six years after, Shelmith realized that Sheila will never give back the money and she was lost in thought not knowing what to do. All this time, Shelmith was praying to God to give her a way out of this, seemingly tricky situation and she trusted that way would be forthcoming.

Not long ago and Shelmith was busy checking her mails and she came across one that was from Sheila. Thinking that finally she was going to tell her that she has paid up the money, she went on to open the mail eagerly.

"I am inviting you over to my house next weekend for a 'women's only recreational fellowship', the mail read. She prepared herself to go over to Sheila's house the following Saturday and since she was attending another conference the following week, she decided to carry enough clothing inform of a luggage and leave it somewhere near the place where she was going so as to pick it later. The only place where she could leave the luggage was at Sheila's husband's office although her plan was to leave it with the secretary.

At Mr. Jones office, Shelmith explained herself to the secretary who was very willing to help.

She showed her where to keep her luggage. To her surprise, when she opened the door, her eyes met with his. She had not planned. She could not turn away and pretend that she had not seen him.

"Hello Mr. Jones?" she greeted him.

"To you too madam, how are you?" he stood to welcome her as he showed her a seat.

"Am good sir. How have you been for many days?" she inquired.

"I've been okay." He said. They continued to exchange pleasantries for some time and when they had talked for some time, Shelmith brought out the issue.

"Mr. Jones am quite ashamed as I talk to you over this matter. This is something that we were supposed to talk about six years back, but I cannot explain why we did not talk about it…"

Mr. Jones nodded in agreement. Shelmith continued.

"You remember the issue of the money. I know until now your wife has never told you what transpired and as much as I begged her to explain to you what happened, I realized she was not ready to tell you so I have decided to do myself." She said.

"I did as we had agreed and I returned your money in two installments, but instead of bringing it directly to you, I would give it over to your wife to hand it over to you. I did the same with the second installment. However, I noted that something was not in order when you did not call to notify me of its reception so after sometime; I called her to ask if she had given you back. She told me that she was going through a rough time, short of finances and therefore she used that money.

Her idea was that after she has been able to recover that money, she would be able to give you back of which she has not happened until now. I had requested her sometimes back to inform you that I had given back and that, she had used the money, but she appears to fear you very much, she was not able to tell you." Shelmith said.

Mr. Jones just smiled back and said, "She is my wife and if she has the money, then I am satisfied. Do not worry anymore about it as I am sure she put it into good use. I normally follow to see the projects that she is undertaking and I am quite impressed with them."

"Whoa! I am so glad to hear that Mr. Jones. You have no idea how relieved I am to hear that. With that, I can happily join the others in your house for the fellowship." Shelmith admitted.

"Oh yes my sister please enjoy yourself and I am happy to meet you after a long long time". Mr. Jones interjected.

"I hope you will join us." She said.

"Well, no. It is good to give you uninterrupted freedom. May God bless you indeed." Said he.

Shelmith left Mr. Jones office quite satisfied and joined the others in Mrs. Jones house. After the fellowship was over and the guests were leaving at their own leisure, Shelmith called Sheila aside and told her what transpired. Sheila was flabbergasted. She did not think that Shelmith would actually do that and Shelmith took time to explain to her why it was important. Sheila understood and really apologized to Shelmith for subjecting her to all that but the day ended well with Shelmith totally vindicated.
2 Corinthians 5:17-18

So, if anyone is in Christ Jesus, he is a new creation, the old has passed away, behold, the new has come. All this is from God, who reconciled us to Himself through Christ, and has given us the ministry of reconciliation.

When we first received Jesus as our savior, two things happened. Immediately, the old was wiped and right away, it was replaced with the new. The old represents our former selves like sins, diseases, poverty, problems and other vices that do not represent the power of God. When Jesus comes into our lives, He exchanges all that with the newness that belongs to Him. He blots away our sins, overcomes diseases and all weaknesses. However, since we are not immediately aware of that, then the old continues to suppress and intimidate us. Therefore, knowledge is power.

Hosea 4:6 says that my people are destroyed for lack of wisdom.

We are destroyed for lack of knowledge.

Sadly, many have remained and are perishing in sin, sicknesses and other bad things simply because they are not aware that Jesus has already paid for that. Many are stuck in debilitating sicknesses for not being aware that they can walk free. Knowledge is power. Like Solomon, let us all emulate him and ask for wisdom.

The second part of the scripture 2 Cor.5:18 say that; all this is from God. The newness we are saying here is from God.

Diabetes is not from God. Financial bankruptcy is also not from God. Nothing evil comes from God. From

God, comes all the good things but we must be aware that he uses them for us to acquire the blessings of God.
God does not exactly want to give us a car, money all those things we feel like we need them. First, He wants to equip us with the knowledge that he is the Lord God of newness.

2Corin. 5:7 advises us *to excel in everything in faith, speech, knowledge, in utmost eagerness and love.*

As we excel in this, then everything else starts to fall in place. During church school, there was one very common chorus we loved singing, "I seek ye first the kingdom of God, and his righteousness, and all the things shall be added unto you, hallelujah, hallelujah".

There is a great danger when we are able to achieve the worldly riches before knowing Christ. No wonder Jesus told the young man in a parable to sell all that he had in order to see the kingdom of God, and the young man declined. Jesus knew that when we start with Him, then success is assured unlike when we starts with riches and then struggle to find him.

My Journey Through a Wilderness

12.
MAINTAINING THE GLORY

There is no greater joy like for that person who has already won all the battles and is now on the other side of victory. I will never forget the joy I had on my graduation day. Having done my studies at the university and finally completing was something to be happy about. The four years of study were like a wilderness, which I had eventually concluded on this happy occasion and celebration. Some of the terrible experiences we go through in life are finally marked with one long and a happy occasion, which signifies that we have finally come through. When I started working, I did it with the confidence of one person who was given the power to read and to do everything that pertains to it. I am not like any other person who has not gone through the process of what I went through. Spiritual wilderness is the same.

Every individual who has gone through some terrible experience stands better than one who has not. That is why; God in His infinite wisdom takes everyone one of us through such although the degree matters. After He has finished with us, He then places us where we can be of use depending on what we have gone through. Today, many church leaders and elders give me sessions to teach their congregations on how to give tithes and offerings. The reason is God has taken me through fire on the same to furnish me with the information and power that He needed me to acquire on the same. Even as He takes me to higher places on the same, I have to continue to be faithful on what He has called me to do. I also find God leading me to speak to many couples especially those who are having misunderstandings amongst themselves. I am able to rely on God for practical insight to bail them out of their troubles. In other words, I am of great use now in the church that when I was just a newbie many years ago. I cannot say that wilderness was good but it helped me to become what I am today. I am also able to preach the Word of God with power because the same was cemented in my life when I was learning to trust in Him. Now the wilderness is over. Glory has already been bestowed on you. How do we maintain the glory? How do we go on winning all the battles that come our way?

Luke 5:1-11

Therefore, it was, as the multitude pressed about Him to hear the word of God that He stood by the Lake of Gennesaret

2 and saw two boats standing by the lake; but the fishermen had gone from them and were washing their nets.

3 Then He got into one of the boats, which was Simon's, and asked him to put out a little from the land. And He sat down and taught the multitudes from the boat.

4 When He had stopped speaking, He said to Simon, "Launch out into the deep and let down your nets for a catch."

5 but Simon answered and said to Him, "Master, we have toiled all night and caught nothing;

nevertheless at Your word I will let down the net."

6 And when they had done this, they caught a great number of fish, and their net was breaking.

7 So they signaled to their partners in the other boat to come and help them. And they came and filled both the boats, so that they began to sink.
8 When Simon Peter saw it, he fell down at Jesus' knees, saying, "Depart from me, for I am a sinful man, O Lord!"
9 For he and all who were with him were astonished at the catch of fish, which they had taken;
10 and so also were James and John, the sons of Zebedee, who were partners with Simon. And Jesus said to Simon, "Do not be afraid. From now on you will catch men."
11 So when they had brought their boats to land, they forsook all and followed Him.
NKJV

This story tells about Simon with the other disciples and they had spent the whole night trying to catch fish. Then, the following day Jesus was teaching a multitude which had followed Him and He lacked a space to stand and address them. Jesus asked Simon to let Him use his boat so that He could move away a bit inside the waters to have a good view if the multitude. When Jesus was through with addressing the people, He told Simon to push the boat further to the deep water and throw the net for a catch. Note the way Simon answered Jesus.

He said, "Master, we worked hard all night long and caught nothing but if you say so, I will let down the nets." They let them down and caught such a large number of fish that the nets were about to break. This passage really surprises me. Jesus does not use anyone's item without paying back for the services. I am obliged to say this; God does not waste an experience. You may go through a tough experience all through waiting upon God's deliverance; He will later use it to bless the lives of other people. Then He does not just return it the way it was but makes it many times better than it was before.

Simon obeyed. What happened next was unbelievable. Simon was actually telling Jesus that at the same spot, they had spent the whole night with no success. That tells us that Jesus is not even the expert here but the master. He caught a large number of fish until the nets were breaking. They simply were not able to lift the nets. Sometimes if a person has suffered financially for a long time, God may perform a breathtaking miracle that makes that person not just a millionaire but also even a billionaire. This act was so marvelous, that Simon fell at Jesus feet and cried to Him saying that he was a sinner. A huge promotion must humble a person. I heard a comment once that most of the rich people are very down to earth fellows. They have nothing to be boastful about.

Jesus told him, that He was going to make Him a fisher of men. Jesus knew that even with a large catch of fish, Simon would soon become restless if he would go fishing again and gets frustrated or even the fact he would get lost in the world of sin with too much of what he was looking for if it was not directed divinely. That is why Jesus had to engage him at this point so that this miracle would bear fruits eventually. Normally, after a big miracle, Jesus must engage a person so that this person becomes of use in His kingdom. It is normally at this point that people become restless and drift further from the will of God. One of my uncles was a very wealthy man in his youth. He owned vast real estate companies and even his children had also acquired the wealth at quite an early age. He never saw the need of giving his life to Christ and chose to remain a quiet churchgoer without really involving himself to deeper church matters. As he grew older, he started becoming restless and unknown to us one time, he planned to commit suicide and end his life. Incidentally, he could not bring himself to do it since he was a respected man in the church and in the circles of his business counterparts.

Therefore, he made a secret plan to fly out to Israel and kill himself in a hotel. In the plane, as he testified to us later on, God asked him in a loud voice where he was going and what he had in mind. It was at that point that he gave his life to Christ and on arrival to Israel; he boarded a flight back to Kenya. He came to testify of the mighty salvation from his own planned death.

Simon later went and followed Jesus. Jesus made him a fisher of men. His wilderness was transformed into a great ministry of soul winning. In every wilderness that we go through, when we commit it to God, He changes it for good. I had said earlier that everything works together for our good. If the devil knew that

God would use it for our good, he would never bother harassing us

mercilessly. I thank God for His word that says, I waited patiently for the Lord, and He made step on a hard place. The psalmist recognizes that, he had been sinking in miry clay, a hopeless situation. But his hope was on God. He never trusted any other to help other than Almighty God. In turn, God did not frustrate his hope and He will never do that to us either. He is always looking out to any of us ready to trust Him so that He can help us too. His word says that His eyes are normally out searching back and forth for any son or daughter out there who is craving for His attention.

••

Some scriptures that help one when in wilderness include:

Psalms 139
1. To the chief Musician, A Psalm of David. O LORD, thou hast searched me, and known [me].
2. Thou knowest my down sitting and mine uprising, thou understandest my thought afar off.
3. Thou compassest my path and my lying down and art acquainted [with] all my ways.
4. For [there is] not a word in my tongue, [but], lo, O LORD, thou knowest it altogether.
5. Thou hast beset me behind and before, and laid thine hand upon me.

6. [Such] knowledge [is] too wonderful for me; it is high, I cannot [attain] unto it.
7. Whither shall I go from thy spirit? or whither shall I flee from thy presence?
8. If I ascend up into heaven, thou [art] there: if I make my bed in hell, behold, thou [art there].
9. [If] I take the wings of the morning, [and] dwell in the uttermost parts of the sea;
10. Even there shall thy hand lead me and thy right hand shall hold me.
11. If I say, Surely the darkness shall cover me; even the night shall be light about me.
12. Yea, the darkness hideth not from thee; but the night shineth as the day: the darkness and the light [are] both alike [to thee].
13. For thou hast possessed my reins: thou hast covered me in my mother's womb.
14. I will praise thee; for I am fearfully [and] wonderfully made: marvellous [are] thy works; and [that] my soul knoweth right well.
15. My substance was not hid from thee, when I was made in secret, [and] curiously wrought in the lowest parts of the earth.
16. Thine eyes did see my substance, yet being imperfect; and in thy book all [my members] were written, [which] in continuance were fashioned, when [as yet there was] none of them.
17. How precious also are thy thoughts unto me, O God! how great is the sum of them!
18. [If] I should count them, they are more in number than the sand: when I awake, I am still with thee.

19. *Surely thou wilt slay the wicked, O God: depart from me therefore, ye bloody men.*
20. *For they speak against thee wickedly [and] thine enemies take [thy name] in vain.*
21. *Do not I hate them, O LORD, that hates thee? and am not I grieved with those that rise up against thee?*
22. *I hate them with perfect hatred: I count them mine enemies.*
23. *Search me, O God, and know my heart: try me, and know my thoughts:*
24. *And see if [there be any] wicked way in me, and lead me in the way everlasting.*

Habakkuk 3:17-19
17. *Although the fig tree shall not blossom, neither [shall] fruit [be] in the vines; the labor of the olive shall fail, and the fields shall yield no meat; the flock shall be cut off from the fold, and [there shall be] no herd in the stalls:*
18. *Yet I will rejoice in the LORD, I will joy in the God of my salvation.*
19. *The LORD God [is] my strength, and he will make my feet like hinds' [feet], and he will make me to walk upon mine high places. To the chief singer on my stringed instruments.*

Isaiah 35
1. *The wilderness and the solitary place shall be glad for them; and the desert shall rejoice and blossom as the rose.*
2. *It shall blossom abundantly, and rejoice even with joy and singing: the glory of Lebanon shall be given unto it, the excellency of Carmel and Sharon, they shall see the glory of the LORD, [and] the excellency of our God.*

3. *Strengthen ye the weak hands, and confirm the feeble knees.*
4. *Say to them [that are] of a fearful heart, Be strong, fear not: behold, your God will come [with] vengeance, [even] God [with] a recompence; he will come and save you.*
5. *Then the eyes of the blind shall be opened, and the ears of the deaf shall be unstopped.*
6. *Then shall the lame [man] leap as a hart, and the tongue of the dumb sing: for in the wilderness shall waters break out, and streams in the desert.*
7. *And the parched ground shall become a pool, and the thirsty land springs of water: in the habitation of dragons, where each lay, [shall be] grass with reeds and rushes.*
8. *And an highway shall be there, and a way, and it shall be called The way of holiness; the unclean shall not pass over it; but it [shall be] for those: the wayfaring men, though fools, shall not err [therein].*
neither 9. No lion shall be there, nor [any] ravenous beast shall go up thereon, it shall not be found there; but the redeemed shall walk [there]:
10. *And the ransomed of the LORD shall return, and come to Zion with songs and everlasting joy upon their heads: they shall obtain joy and gladness, and sorrow and sighing shall flee away*
Isaiah 43
1. *But now thus saith the LORD that created thee, O Jacob, and he that formed thee, O Israel, Fear not: for I have redeemed thee, I have called [thee] by thy name; thou [art] mine.*
2. *When thou passest through the waters, I [will be] with thee; and through the rivers, they shall not overflow thee:*

when thou walkest through the fire, thou shalt not be burned; neither shall the flame kindle upon thee.
3. For I [am] the LORD thy God, the Holy One of Israel, thy Savior: I gave Egypt [for] thy ransom, Ethiopia and Seba for thee.
4. Since thou wast precious in my sight, thou hast been honorable, and I have loved thee: therefore will I give men for thee, and people for thy life.
5. Fear not: for I [am] with thee: I will bring thy seed from the east, and gather thee from the west
6. I will say to the north, Give up; and to the south, Keep not back: bring my sons from far, and my daughters from the ends of the earth;
7. [Even] every one that is called by my name: for I have created him for my glory, I have formed him; yea, I have made him.
8. Bring forth the blind people that have eyes and the deaf that have ears.
9. Let all the nations be gathered together, and let the people be assembled: who among them can declare this, and shew us former things? let them bring forth their witnesses, that they may be justified: or let them hear, and say, [It is] truth.
10. Ye [are] my witnesses, saith the LORD, and my servant whom I have chosen: that ye may know and believe me, and understand that I [am] he: before me there was no God formed, neither shall there be after me.
11. I, [even] I, [am] the LORD; and beside me [there is] no savior.

12. I have declared, and have saved, and I have shewed, when [there was] no strange [god] among you: therefore ye [are] my witnesses, saith the LORD, that I [am] God.
13. Yea, before the day [was] I [am] he; and [there is] none that can deliver out of my hand: I will work, and who shall let it?
14. Thus saith the LORD, your redeemer, the Holy One of Israel; For your sake I have sent to Babylon, and have brought down all their nobles, and the Chaldeans, whose cry [is] in the ships.
15. I [am] the LORD, your Holy One, the creator of Israel, your King.
16. Thus saith the LORD, which maketh a way in the sea, and a path in the mighty waters;
17. Which bringeth forth the chariot and horse, the army and the power; they shall lie down together, they shall not rise: they are extinct, they are quenched as tow.
18. Remember ye not the former things, neither consider the things of old.
19. Behold, I will do a new thing; now it shall spring forth; shall ye not know it? I will even make a way in the wilderness, [and] rivers in the desert.
20. The beast of the field shall honor me, the dragons and the owls: because I give waters in the wilderness, [and] rivers in the desert, to give drinks to my people, my chosen.
21. This people have I formed for myself; they shall shew forth my praise.
22. But thou hast not called upon me, O Jacob; but thou hast been weary of me, O Israel.
23. Thou hast not brought me the small cattle of thy burnt offerings; neither hast thou honored me with thy sacrifices.

I have not caused thee to serve with an offering, nor wearied thee with incense.

24. Thou hast bought me no sweet cane with money, neither hast thou filled me with the fat of thy sacrifices: but thou hast made me to serve with thy sins, thou hast wearied me with thine iniquities.

25. I, [even] I, [am] he that blotteth out thy transgressions for mine own sake, and will not remember thy sins.

26. Put me in remembrance: let us plead together: declare thou, that thou mayest be justified.

27. Thy first father hath sinned, and thy teachers have transgressed against me.

28. Therefore I have profaned the princes of the sanctuary, and have given Jacob to the curse, and Israel to reproaches.

A prayer for those in the wilderness

Our Father in heaven,
Hear this prayer we pray,
We commit all those, this day,
that are in various forms of wilderness
that You will grant unto them
the amazing grace from heaven
that even if they are not sure of overcoming
You will take them a step at a time
Day by day
Till they see the end of the tunnel

We pray for the provision
Of the guardian angel
Who will talk to them

In that soft encouraging voice

Help them dear Father
To understand the reason for their wilderness
So that Lord
They will persevere in grace
As they go through this hard time

We pray for grace
We pray for care
We pray for guidance
We pray for mercy
We pray for all their needs
Amen

Paul's special testimony

2 Tim 4:7-8
I have fought a good fight, I have finished [my] course, and I have kept the faith:
8. Henceforth there is laid up for me a crown of righteousness, which the Lord, the righteous judge, shall give me at that day: and not to me only, but unto all them also that love his appearing
Paul knew that the time of his death was drawing near. As he spoke, he used three phrases to sum up his life;
  - I have fought a good fight.
  -I have finished my course.
  - I have kept the faith.

I have fought a good fight
The Christian life is a battle against demonic forces, temptation, the flesh, and the lust of the world. It is recorded in Eph 6:12 that, *For we wrestle not against flesh and blood, but against principalities, against powers, against the rulers of the darkness of this world, against spiritual wickedness in high [places.*
1 john 2; 15-17 also says *Love not the world, neither the things [that are] in the world. If any man love the world, the love of the Father is not in him.*
16. For all that [is] in the world, the lust of the flesh, and the lust of the eyes, and the pride of life, is not of the Father, but is of the world.
17. And the world passeth away, and the lust thereof: but he that doeth the will of God abideth for ever.
Paul had fought a good fight and had been faithful. This clearly tells us that being a successful Christian is not bread and butter. It takes effort. However, it's by God's power that we use to overcome. That is why Paul could say it was not him living in him (Gal 2:20). Our efforts must be to stay dependent on Christ. As we achieve this, the Holy Spirit infuses us with victorious power. Paul states that it was a good fight. The reason is that the outcome was guaranteed. Jesus has already conquered all our foes for us, and all we have to do is stand in His victory. That makes the Christian life a good fight.
I have finished my course
This is comparing life to running a race. Phil 3:13-14

Brethren, I count not myself to have apprehended: but [this] one thing [I do], forgetting those things which are behind, and reaching forth unto those things which are before,
14. I press toward the mark for the prize of the high calling of God in Christ Jesus

He described this race and said that one of the keys to winning is forgetting the things that are behind and focusing on the prize that is ahead. Paul certainly did that. He forsook everything for the rewards the Lord laid in front of him.

<u>I have kept the faith</u>
Paul kept the faith and did not move away from the hope of the Gospel. Col 1:23 states that *If ye continue in the faith grounded and settled, and [be] not moved away from the hope of the gospel, which ye have heard, [and] which was preached to every creature which is under heaven; whereof I Paul am made a minister. As a result,* ''*a crown of righteousness*'' awaited him as we see in 2Tim 4:8
Henceforth there is laid up for me a crown of righteousness, which the Lord, the righteous judge, shall give me at that day: and not to me only, but unto all them also that love his appearing.

Paul's testimony serves as an encouragement to us and also to those who are going through some wilderness. It is a special reminder that every wilderness has an exit door, every problem has its expiry date and that every tear has one who wipes it.

13.
CONCLUSION

Many people are out there struggling in various kinds of problems. Whatever it is that is your wilderness today, dare to turn to God and eventually you will experience the mighty touch of Jesus? It is not over until Jesus says it is over. I have personally gone through very traumatizing situations in my life, but with the help of the Almighty God, I never at once looked back or sought help from anywhere else apart from God and He in turn was very faithful to me. I can testify that He picked me from zero and He is taking me step by step to becoming a hero.

Advantages of a wilderness experience include;
*One is humbled;
 *One has a greater confidence and reliance on God;

*One can also lose some friends; and
*One attains a greater and refined character.

The wilderness is a place between you and the manifestation of God's promise in your life. Until you embrace and enjoy the wilderness; your ability to handle God's best for you is, at best, weak and incomplete. Let God have His way with and in you. Accept this invitation to the wilderness.
It is only those who are *sweetly broken* by God in the wilderness who understand, appreciate, and truly know His *love*, *power*, and *grace*!

My personal testimony.

I give God all the glory. I have gone through terrible situations but God has restored me fully, I serve God with a lot of zeal because I understand that He was preparing me to become better acquainted with His work. He restored my marriage. My husband is the

best thing that happened to me. He is sweet and loving and very understanding too. God has restored my finances too. I am able to serve Him with it. I have also been promoted severally in my place of work. There are so many countless blessings that I cannot talk about here.
May God bless you.

www.ingramcontent.com/pod-product-compliance
Lightning Source LLC
Chambersburg PA
CBHW050322120526
44592CB00014B/2019